W9-DCG-444

Dear Vicky

Hope this is of a bit of use as you begin your ministry at Walnut Hill

In gospel partnership

Andrew

The because approach.
Innovating church for all.

Let me tell you why I heartily recommend Andrew Baughen's book on evangelism, *The Because Approach. Innovating Church For All*. It is deeply rooted in Scripture and in contemporary culture. It draws from his twofold experience in the city and in the parish. It combines solid theory about strategy with his realistic six-stage plan. And it comes out of a heart passionately committed to Christ, the gospel and the local church. I cannot imagine that any individual or church group could study it without being profoundly challenged and inspired.
John Stott

This book is driven by a passion for the glory of God in the proclamation of the gospel to needy outsiders. It is biblically informed and robustly practical, and many church leaders will benefit from its wisdom.
Christopher Ash, Director, the Cornhill Training Course

Finally, in a 'one-size-fits all, formula for success, if only you do it this way' culture, a book that takes you through a step-by-step approach to discerning God's purposes for YOUR church in YOUR context with YOUR people. Andrew Baughen has given us a method of planning strategically that is biblical, practical and workable. Read it with your church leaders to discover how you can grow healthy disciples and a healthy church. You may not agree with all of it - but you will be forced to think through WHY you do what you do as a church, and whether you could do things better. A book that gives you the 'so what?' answers to the questions of why you need to think strategically.
Dave Richards, St Paul's and St George's, Edinburgh

This book cuts you open. I found it confronted me with realities from the Bible, from my local church and from the culture. Page after page provokes careful reflection.
Rico Tice, Curate, All Souls Church, London

Of the many books I have read on evangelism Andrew Baughen's is one of the best. It is biblical, lively, and contextually savvy. His key points are right on target, namely that evangelism needs to be continuous, represent the heartbeat of congregational life, and be focused not only on bringing people to a point of initial commitment to Jesus but to become Christ-followers who are making a difference in the world.
Eddie Gibbs, Fuller Seminary, Pasadena

A thought-provoking book that would have been really helpful when I started the Net Church seven years ago. It deals with so many of the issues I had to grapple with.
Dave Male, Vicar, the Net Church, Huddersfield, an Anglican 'network church'

The contents of *The Because Approach* complement the strategic work with churches that we are pioneering in England and Wales. The book will inspire and equip churches as they seek to make Jesus the centre of their church strategy.
Pauline Burdett, Family Ministry Project Manager, Scripture Union England and Wales

Andrew Baughen has written an eminently helpful book that combines a biblical understanding of ministry with practical suggestions stemming from years of experience in revitalizing a center-city church. Hurrah!
Al Barth, European Coordinator for Church Planting, Redeemer Church Planting Center, associated with Redeemer Presbyterian Church, Manhattan, New York

The Because Approach demonstrates the power of a good question. By asking and answering the 'so what?' question at all the right moments Andrew provides a highly effective tool for any church leadership that's passionate about bringing focus and energy to their mission agenda.
Tracy Cotterell, Imagine Project Director, London Institute of Contemporary Christianity

Reconnecting with the Bible is the source of authentic renewal and *The Because Approach* starts with Scripture but helps us to a fresh eye by drawing parallels from popular culture and especially from films. The result is a course which teaches practical wisdom about how to grow a local Christian community. The particular value of *The Because Approach* is that it has been written by someone who has followed his own advice and tried his own method in a fruitful ministry in Clerkenwell.
Richard Chartres, Bishop of London

Thinking strategically about the mission of the church is vital. Not only does this book give a biblical and practical tool for doing this, it also offers thoughtful and incisive ideas that will make a difference. Buy this book. Use it. It could change your church.
James Lawrence, Director of Arrow Leadership Programme, CPAS

It is essential today that churches are aware of what they are meant to be doing as they organise themselves around the task of making disciples for the Lord Jesus. So I am thrilled with *The Because Approach*: gospel driven, evangelistically passionate, warm hearted, culturally relevant, and – above all – practical and achievable strategies for us to be the people Christ wants us to be.
Chris Green, Vice Principal, Oak Hill College

Many books offer to solve the 'how' questions of local church growth, but never address the 'why'. Andrew Baughen's lively handbook is bursting with creative ideas and practical suggestions for churches and individuals, but they are all grounded in a comprehensive rationale that takes the biblical worldview and contemporary culture with the seriousness they both deserve.
Chris Wright, Langham Partnership International

This is exactly the kind of book we need right now that can help us engage with new ways of being Church. It is from someone who has put his ideas to the test and knows what can work. Andrew has done us a great service. This is a superb book that should be read by all who are concerned about the mission of the church.

Wallace Benn, Bishop of Lewes

The Bible's term 'wisdom' describes an approach to life that is intensely practical and profoundly theological. Wisdom shows you the best life to live before God. The term 'strategy' describes the same thing: what to do in the world when you acknowledge that God is God. Andrew Baughen's book is about church strategy, about a wise life for the fellowship. *Because* is bursting with ideas that overflow from great theology. A multitude of useful suggestions arise from the 'big picture' of the gospel of our gracious King of Love. 'Try this because God is like that'. The strategic steps that Andrew lays out for God's mission through the local church are applicable to any fellowship, of any size, in any place and at any stage in its life. They have already helped our fellowship enormously, and I've only read the draft. Brilliant!

Dominic Smart, Gilcomston South Church, Aberdeen

Each time we gather for worship we ask our people to pray 'your kingdom come, your will be done' but don't always have much of a clue how we as a church might become part of the answer. Andrew's clear analysis and infectious enthusiasm will help every church cut through the fog of daily life and be strategic in doing church. As a church who trialled Andrew's material with him we found the ideas incredibly helpful in focusing our energy effectively. This book will demand careful study and application. Why? 'Because you're worth it.'

Martyn Saunders, All Saints, King's Cross, London

The because approach.
Innovating church for all.

BECAUSE B

Copyright © 2005 Andrew Baughen

11 10 09 08 07 06 05 7 6 5 4 3 2 1

First published 2005 by Authentic Media
9 Holdom Avenue, Bletchley, Milton Keynes, Bucks, MK1 1QR, UK
and 129 Mobilization Drive, Waynesboro, GA 30830-4575, USA
www.authenticmedia.co.uk
Authentic Media is a division of Send The Light Ltd., a company limited by guarantee
(registered charity no. 270162)

The right of Andrew Baughen to be identified as the Author of this Work has been asserted
by him in accordance with the Copyright, Designs and Patents Act 1988.

All rights reserved. No part of this publication may be reproduced,
stored in a retrieval system, or transmitted in any form or
by any means, electronic, mechanical, photocopying, recording or
otherwise, without the prior permission of the publisher or a licence
permitting restricted copying. In the UK such licences are issued by the
Copyright Licensing Agency.
90 Tottenham Court Road, London, W1P 9HE

British Library Cataloguing in Publication Data

A catalogue record for this book is available from the British Library

ISBN 1-85078-614-3

Unless otherwise stated, Scripture quotations are taken from the
HOLY BIBLE, NEW INTERNATIONAL VERSION
Copyright © 1973, 1978, 1984 by the International Bible Society. Used by permission of
Hodder & Stoughton Limited. All rights reserved. 'NIV' is a registered trademark of the
international Bible Society. UK trademark number 1448790

Cover and layout design by David Norton, Anderson Norton Design, Clerkenwell
Photos: Cover © Getty Images.   Pages 2, 8, 18, 70, 96, 155 © Andrew Baughen
Pages 38, 127 by W.G.Briggs © Andrew Baughen

Printed in Great Britain by Bell & Bain Ltd., Glasgow

Praise God who has blessed me with every spiritual blessing in Christ. To Rachel, my remarkable omni-competent wife who I love and who proves each day that it is possible to build a marriage even when your husband is a sinner like me. To Charlotte, my radiant older daughter of whom I'm very proud and who proves that you don't need to be over 18 to be a church planting missionary – keep going, girl! To Harriet, my sparkly younger daughter of whom I'm also very proud and whose discipline of Bible study, prayer and personal evangelism is a great example to me – keep growing, girl! To Dad, thank you for giving me a passion for Christ and his church – Jesus be pre-eminent! To Mum, thank you for giving me constant unconditional love – I don't know where I'd be without you! To my sister Rachel, thank you for being a sister I could look up to as I was growing up and learn from – respect! To my brother Philip, thank you for being a big brother who always protected and supported me – you win! **In my development as a Christian disciple.** To the dorm leader who encouraged me to turn to Jesus from just a figure in my life to my friend for life eternal. To Mary Hollingshead and many others who've consistently prayed for me. To Uncle John Stott, who is my role model of godliness (outside of the Bible!). To Nigel and Jan Skelsey, who included me as a friend when I was an awkward teenager. To Andrew Cornes, who taught me 'The Basic Method' of Bible study and the practice of appreciation. To Mike and Claire Lawson, who introduced me to Rachel. To Kim Swithinbank, who gave me my first taste of mission. To Steve Wookey, who trusted me to start preaching. To Jonathan Fletcher, who taught me the role of the pastor teacher. To Rico Tice, who showed me what it looks like to be an evangelist. To Paul Perkin, who encouraged me even when I did him wrong. To Jamie Colman, who assured me often that I wasn't mad. To Andy Mossop, who suggested I take up movie making as chill therapy. To Raj Parker, who reminds me frequently that the gospel is the power of God for salvation. To David Picton Turbervill, who taught me the value of long-term friendship. To Caroline Hanwell, who showed me that coming to faith is a long journey that's worth every step. To Peter Froggatt, David Williams, James Robson and Simon Austen, who've encouraged me to keep going in ministry. To John Pearce, my mentor. **In my work as a strategy consultant.** To Angus Hislop, who gave me my break as a management consultant. To Elizabeth Corley, thank you for being a discerning boss and for continuing to care about me. To Nigel Taverner, who taught me strategy consulting and to ask 'so what'. To Nicholas Beasley, who was not only my manager but also cared enough to invest in me, challenge me and befriend me. **In my work at St James Clerkenwell.** To John Fitt, Annie Wyatt, Bishop Richard Chartres and Bishop John Sentamu, who trusted me to reboot JC-Church. To Rachel's mum and dad for supporting us in many ways. To all the JC Partners who've come over the years and served for a season and/or stayed as part of the family – your work prompted by love will last for eternity and is much appreciated. To an amazing staff team over the years (Nick, Jo, Martin, Dan, Tim, Ben, Kay, Luke, Nick, Hugh, Jenny, Philippa, Peter, Felicity, Sheila, Francis, Tim, Glen, Emma, Rachel, Andy, Simon, Amy, Ruth, John Mark, Francis, Rebecca, Kathie) who've given more and coped with me more than should be reasonably expected – thank you for your gospel partnership. To Richard Coekin, who generously shared his ministry trainees with us. To all the people I've married. To Emma Gerrard for making me laugh. To all the people who've come to know Christ at JC – you're an amazing joy! To Mark and Lee Taylor, thank you for staying committed and incredibly supportive when so many friends were moving on. To James Pollard, thank you for being a mate in so many ways. To Mel and John Butler, thank you for including our family in yours. To David Norton, thank you for not just being a brilliant designer but also a friend – keep seeking Christ! **In my work on the Because Approach.** To Bill Hybels, who first inspired me to have a big and clear vision for what a church can be. To Mark Mittelberg and Wayne Alguire, who gave me time on my visits to Willow and to Anne and Fred Huetter, Joe and Lois Adamczyk and many others who showed such generous hospitality. To Tim Keller for inspiring me with a vision for the city. To Al Barth, Tuck Bartholomew and Scott Strickman for giving me time on my visits to Manhattan. To Steve Beck who speaks the same strategy language. To the 1995 St Marks Battersea Rise staff team who jointly thought up the stadium model. To Mark Finnie and Charlotte Hubback – thank you for asking me to produce this. To Stephen Williams, Bishop Stephen Oliver, Lyle Dennen and Sion College for support and helping fund the research. To Dotty Larson, who not only provided a place for me to study but also a life of devotion to God for me to copy. To Rick Warren for sharing ideas. To James Lawrence, my writing partner in the early stages and an example of godliness to me. To Ian Barnetson for giving initial advice, Philip Sudell for offering consistently brilliant criticism, Elizabeth Roberts for making amendments and Janet Heppell and Kay and Guy Carter for checking the detail. To Mark McKee and Yo-Hahn Low for designing the website. To Mark Greene, Tracy Cotterell and Nick Spencer at LICC for sharing advice and ideas. To all the others who've given input – especially Nicky Gumbel, J.John, Mike Hill, Chris Green and Dave Mayle. **And finally.** To Tara Smith, who is far more than an editor – more of a sounding board, adviser and encourager – Live and Let Deadlines!

Above my desk I have a poster of the film *Lost in Translation* which has the following strap line across the top: 'everyone wants to be found'. It keeps reminding me of the great commission Jesus has given his church – to help people who are lost in a mistranslation of God's eternal truth.

This book comes out of 3 convictions about the local church:

1. The local church is the hope for a world lost in mistranslation.
The church is God's treasured possession – a bright city on a hill declaring the praises of him who calls people out of darkness.

2. Each local church carries out its divine commission to a lost world backed by the personal guarantee of Jesus Christ that his church will prevail.
Proof of that guarantee can be found in London's Clerkenwell where a Christian church has prevailed since 1100. I arrived 897 years into the venture when the numbers were relatively small but the confidence in Christ's plan for local churches was still very much alive. The certainty in Christ as church builder was reinforced by a mandate from the patrons and bishop to start again with something fresh and new – what's known as a 'church reboot'.

3. Each local church carries out the same commission to reach lost people but does that within a unique situation.
One thing is certain – any one church that puts into practice every activity, programme and initiative available or suggested in this book would be a church on the way to nervous melt-down!

This book is a six-step strategic review process for a church.
It aims to help each local church:

1. Be the hope for a world lost in mistranslation, a church that knows how to present the unchanging truth of Christ crucified in a language our lost world can understand.

2. Be a prevailing church that has confidence in plans founded on the Bible's timeless first principles.

3. Be a contextual church that knows which activities should be the focus of attention, which shouldn't and why.

CONTENTS

Introducing. The because approach.

step 1. Preparation.

step 2. Relationship building.

step 3. Respect building.

step 4. Relevance building.

step 5. Response building.

step 6. Participation.

Jeremiah 29:11
'For I know the plans I have for you,'
declares the LORD,
'plans to prosper you and not to harm you,
plans to give you hope and a future.'

Introducing.
The because approach.

'Because the Bible tells me so.'

The because approach.

In the film *Jerry Maguire*[1], the title character is a sports agent who wakes up in the middle of the night to the realization that in all the rush of life he's lost sight of the simple pleasures of the job and why he chose the line of work in the first place. He says: 'With so many clients, we had forgotten what was important.' We can be a bit like that – we can become frenetically busy without necessarily knowing why we're doing all the things we're doing. The Because Approach restores the 'why' so that every person involved in every activity can fill in the sentence 'I'm doing this because...' and 'I'm not doing that because...'

Back in my days as a strategy consultant, there were two words my boss would consistently write on presentations I'd prepared – 'so what?' It's a great question to ask. You may be involved in lots of activities, but can you answer the 'so what' behind them? The Because Approach helps us identify and articulate the 'so what' – the purpose behind all that we do.

Innovating church for all.

In 2004, the Discrimination Disability Act came into effect in the UK. It is now against the law for a public building not to provide access for all to their facilities. Will your church provide access for all to your gospel facilities? Are there spiritually disabled people, cut off from access to God, for whom you are not providing help? Are you taking seriously the DDA legislation of the King to make disciples of all nations?

At the birth of Jesus, the angel announced good news of great joy for all people. Jesus himself is clear that he is the Messiah of all people and calls all people everywhere to repent. The Because Approach is about innovating church so all people everywhere can hear Christ's call to receive eternal life.

The because approach.

Who is it for?

The Because Approach is for anyone involved in a local church in whatever capacity who has a passion to develop clear biblical, contextual and intentional plans for their church. The principles can equally be applied to a small or large church (the approach was developed at St James Clerkenwell from a starting point of less than 30 adults on Sundays). The approach doesn't assume any particular church setting but is designed to help you analyse your specific situation whatever and wherever that is.

The Because Approach is a tool you can use to discern God's solutions for your church. Whether you are planting a brand new church, developing a fresh expression of church, establishing a new congregation, 'rebooting' an existing church with a new strategy for growth or simply wanting to clarify what you could be doing better, the Because Approach will help you articulate a strategy.

Innovating church for all.

The first in a series of
because approach guides.

The because approach.

How does it work?

This book is designed to excite, inform, remind, provoke and thoroughly ignite your imagination of what your church could be.

To help navigation of the material, each of the six steps is split into sections.
– If you prefer to start with all the biblical backing you could begin by reading the 'scripture' sections at the start of each step.
– If you like to set up the issue first you could start with the six 'setting' sections.
– If you want to cut to the action you could work back from the six 'solutions' sections.

To help ease of use, each double page spread is an inherent piece of writing.
– You could simply read one double page spread per day.
– You could dip in and out of it when you are looking for a bit of inspiration.
Whichever way you use the book, it is well worth reading in short spurts with plenty of time to think through the implications.

To help group study, each step ends with a study guide.
– Some churches may use the six studies in specific leadership teams or more widely across their network of small groups.
– The six-part course could be studied over six weeks or six months.
– Each participant prepares for the group meeting by reading the chapter under consideration, and the group then meets to discuss the material using the study guide.

Other hints
A 'handout version' of the study guide is downloadable at www.becauseapproach.com.

Each chapter includes suggestions for research in your particular context that will help you through this process. To ease the workload for study groups, some of this legwork can be done in advance.

In the future, the website (www.becauseapproach.com) will have case studies, updates on further solutions and links to more resources which will help you develop solutions appropriate in your setting. Your contributions will be gratefully received.

Also listed on the website are notes and resources for people who want to run the Because Approach as a course in their church.

The Because Approach asks three questions about everything we do:

What is the biblical reason for doing this activity?

How do the opportunities and challenges of our present situation shape our biblical mandate?

What activities will fulfil the mandate of Scripture within the setting to which we are called?

SCRIPTURE

SETTING

SOLUTION

3

Scripture: 'Because the Bible says...'

The Bible is a lamp that lights up the path we should follow (Ps. 119:105). So if we want to answer the question 'why should we do this?' we first need to ask 'what does the Bible say about this?' The Because Approach begins by asking the 'biblical why' of every step we take and every activity we undertake:

– 'Why do I do this?' 'Because the Bible says...'
– 'Why does the Bible say...?' 'Because...'

With the Because Approach we are able to establish foundation values that will underpin every good work (2 Tim. 3:16–17). It's those biblical values that will transform an activity into a God-given ministry. The Bible's values will also determine how we undertake an activity and how much people get involved in it. A sound biblical 'because' will inspire people to say, 'I will give my time and energy to this ministry because it's of great value to my Lord.'

SCRIPTURE
SETTING
SOLUTION
3

Setting: 'Because our context is...'

The Bible thoroughly equips every Christian for every good work but does not give us a specific blueprint for how to implement any given activity. Our particular situation in space and time will focus a universal biblical injunction into a specific vision for us. That's why the second question the Because Approach asks is: 'how does our present situation shape our Bible mandate?' Our context is made up of four classic elements: our strengths, weaknesses, opportunities and threats. We need to look at the positive aspects of our situation as well as the barriers we face.

1 Corinthians 7 reminds us that while our situation may be far from ideal, it's the reality we're called to at the present time. As a result, however difficult our context might be, we can always choose to do what counts: keeping God's commands (1 Cor. 7:19). Everybody is called to do something, but nobody is called to do everything. Jesus moved on from one village to another before all the sick were healed because he did not come to bring physical healing to everyone. Simply, he applied the purpose for which he'd come to every decision he made and every action he accomplished.

The Because Approach enables us to discern our specific calling. It helps us answer the questions 'why me?' and 'why now?' by applying biblically grounded principles to our divinely given situation and abilities. The resulting vision enables us to know clearly why we undertake an activity and who gets involved. 'We do this because God has placed us in this exciting situation and equipped us to take hold of this important opportunity.'

SCRIPTURE
SETTING
SOLUTION

3

Solution: 'Because we've agreed a plan...'

Once we are clear what the Bible says and what the opportunities and limits of our context are, we then need to agree what to do. The most accurate exegesis of the original Bible manuscripts and the highest level of glossy full-colour graphic all-singing contextual analysis is just dead weight without action.

The Because Approach helps us answer the questions 'why do we do what we do?' and 'why do we do it like that?' The answer to the first question will be a combination of 'because the Bible tells us to do it' and 'because our context creates an opportunity for it in the following ways...' The answer to 'why do we do it like that?' may be 'because the Bible teaches us to do it like that' or 'because that's what's appropriate in our context' or simply 'because out of all the biblical and contextually appropriate possibilities, that's what we've decided!' After all, there's rarely one right answer to a problem but there's usually benefit in sticking to one solution.

The Because Approach generates biblical reasons for Christian action in specific situations. It shows us how to turn our reactive approach to planning into a proactive approach. With this approach we agree action plans together that look forward to a future position rather than back to past traditions.

Proverbs 19:21
Many are the plans in a human's heart,
but it is the LORD's purpose that prevails.
(TNIV)

step **1**.

Preparation.

'Because behind every great plan
there's got to be a great intention.'

In the film *Gladiator*, Caesar knows he's old and death is imminent. So he calls his most trusted general, Maximus, to come to him. Caesar tells Maximus, 'When a man sees his end he wants to know there was some purpose to his life .' Caesar's purpose is the dream of Rome. As he goes on to say, 'There was once a dream of Rome. You could only whisper it. Anything more than a whisper and it would vanish... Maximus, let us whisper now, together, you and I.'

There was once a dream of church – the church in Jerusalem. The people were full of devotion to God and each other and many others heard the whisper and joined them. Our church, too, can make this dream a reality. We can be a people:
– Who know where we're heading and what we're doing
– Of deliberate intention and vision
– Built by Jesus into a church that prevails.
Christ wants to build a prevailing church with the very same mission and vision in your community.
Let's whisper the dream together and keep the dream alive.

In the film *Simon Birch*[3], Simon is a little boy who's different from others in almost every way. At one point, Simon's Sunday School teacher takes him aside and tells him, 'people like you don't belong here'. In fact, what doesn't belong in church is an attitude like that!

The first challenge as we prepare to innovate our church for all is to rediscover Christ's attitude to his church and make that the foundation of all we plan and do.

The New Testament uses the word 'church', which simply means 'an assembly', in a variety of settings. So what is special about a church gathering? What makes church different from the people gathering at the golf club on Sunday morning or the football club on Saturday afternoon or the nightclub on Friday evening?

Church isn't a culturally-controlled invention for 'people like us', it's a divinely-created intention for all who know Jesus

Because Jesus builds his church through us

We love to create new things and we have a tendency to look down on old ideas because we assume they are outmoded and won't be half as exciting. But the reality of building a church is that it's based on practices first tested in ancient Rome and on the principles of someone who was around before time began.

The principles of church growth are as old as the hills, but that doesn't mean we're not to adapt those principles in our own time and place.

Psalm 127
1 Unless the LORD builds the house, its builders labour in vain. Unless the LORD watches over the city, the watchmen stand guard in vain.

Planning is about co-operating with Jesus
1. Christ brings the growth:
– Jesus will build his church (Matt. 16:18)
– God makes churches grow (1 Cor. 3:6).
2. But we are called to be Christ's co-workers:
– Jesus apportions grace to us to build up his church (Eph. 4)
– We plant and water as God's fellow-workers (1 Cor. 3:6, 9).
Preparing a strategic plan, therefore, isn't about usurping Jesus as the Master Builder. It's about co-operating with him as we follow his intended growth plan for our church.

Psalm 40
5 Many, O LORD my God, are the wonders you have done. The things you planned for us no-one can recount to you; were I to speak and tell of them, they would be too many to declare.

Planning is about following Jesus' example
Jesus didn't go through his day randomly, reacting to any and every situation that came his way. He knew what he was and was not called to do each day, and therefore he made a beeline for some situations and positively avoided others. At the beginning of Mark's Gospel we see Jesus under huge pressure and facing demands at every turn. He worked through the pressure by getting up early before the demands hit him, speaking to his heavenly Father and remembering his calling – and then forming a plan as to how he could most effectively fulfil his calling that day (Mark 1:35–39).

The Greek word we translate 'church' is ecclesia. In the New Testament the word is simply used to mean an assembly. So, for example, in Acts 2:32 a riot was brewing in the local stadium and Luke writes that the ecclesia was in confusion. Again in verses 38 and 39, the court is referred to as the ecclesia. Church, therefore, is a non-religious word – what does that teach us about our use of the word?

Planning is about obeying Jesus' command to be strategic

Jesus taught his disciples to be strategic. For example, when he sends them out to teach and heal he tells them:
– Where to go: villages where the population is concentrated
– What to do when they get there: find the 'man of peace' and strategically invest time with him first (Lk. 10:1–18).

'I am sending you out like sheep among wolves. Therefore be as shrewd as snakes and as innocent as doves.' (Matt. 10:16)

Planning is about taking responsibility for what God gives

Planning honours God by using wisely the resources of time, money and energy that he gives. The parable of the talents (Matt. 25:14–28) gives an example of how we are called to use wisely what God has entrusted to us. We, who are 'God's workmanship', need to discern the 'good works, which God prepared in advance for us to do' (Eph. 2:10).

The solutions that different people develop (based on the same scriptural principles and in similar settings) may vary. Although there is often more than one right answer to a problem, the key is to agree something biblical and sensible and then go for it!

Planning is about engaging with God's growth plans

Planning begins and ends with prayer:
– It's about discerning God's calling for us and our church
– It's about trusting God's power to build our church.

Because churches fulfil Christ's two-fold mandate

What makes a church gathering different from a social club?

God's church is unique because it's a gathering of people:
– Who belong to one heavenly Father (Eph. 2:19)
– Whose foundation is one Lord, Jesus Christ
(Eph. 2:20–21)
– In whom God lives by his one Spirit (Eph. 2:22).

God's church is also unique because it a gathering of eternal people of purpose. The first 'church' gathering was the assembly of God's people in the desert at Mount Sinai (Exod. 19:17). Deuteronomy 10:4 describes that landmark event as 'the day of the assembly', and in the New Testament Stephen describes that same desert assembly as the day of the 'ecclesia' – the Greek word for church (Acts 7:38). At the first church they may not have projected slides on a screen, but they did gather to hear and learn the word of God. Church has always been about God's people gathering to hear from him – in that sense, church is an expression of heaven right here on earth.

The church building challenge is the same as it ever was. It is to build a local gathering of God's eternal people who share a clearly defined and firmly held purpose.

All churches have an underlying purpose – even if it's just to do the bare minimum. The question is whether all church members know why the church exists and whether that purpose is worth being a part of.

The Great Commission, with which Jesus leaves his church, sums up the twin purposes that are to be at the heart of every church and are definitely worth giving your life to:
'Therefore go and make disciples...teaching them to obey everything I have commanded you.' (Matt. 28:19–20)

Matthew 16
18 And I tell you that you are Peter, and on this rock I will build my church, and the gates of Hades will not overcome it.

Jeremiah 29
11 'For I know the plans I have for you,' declares the LORD, 'plans to prosper you and not to harm you, plans to give you hope and a future.'

Sara, a young mum who lives on a local estate, was invited to the church toddler group by a friend. Since then she's heard the gospel explained and accepted Christ for herself. As she said in a service recently, 'When Andrew played a clip [from *The Bodyguard*] of Whitney Houston singing "Yes, Jesus loves me" I realized, "yes and he loves me too."' Her partner also became a Christian soon afterwards. They are now married and, with their children, play a key part in the assembly of God's people in Clerkenwell, hearing God's word together and then acting on what they hear. Recently she said publicly, 'When I come to church I feel like I've come home.'

Now that's what I call church!

The apostle Paul identifies the same purposes for the church:
What, after all, is Apollos? And what is Paul? Only servants, through whom you came to believe – as the Lord has assigned to each his task. I planted the seed, Apollos watered it, but God made it grow. (1 Corinthians 3:5-6)

The Because Approach is based on these two purposes: making disciples and maturing disciples.
The church encourages people on the journey of faith by telling them about Jesus. The cross is the changeover point on the journey, where God brings someone from death to life. The church then helps people to develop a deeper and more mature faith.

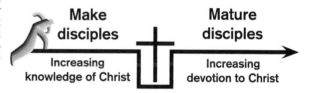

Make disciples | **Mature disciples**

Increasing knowledge of Christ | Increasing devotion to Christ

'Therefore go and make disciples of all nations, baptising them in the name of the Father and of the Son and of the Holy Spirit... (Matt. 28:19)

...and teaching them to obey everything I have commanded you. And surely I am with you always, to the very end of the age.' (Matt. 28:20)

From the start, Jesus taught his disciples to do as he did: to go from village to village and proclaim the good news of the kingdom.
That's how disciples are made: they hear the good news and God brings them into his kingdom of forgiven followers.

Jesus is clear that life change doesn't end with baptism – that's just the beginning. Jesus defines a disciple as someone who not only knows his words but also obeys everything he commands – a challenge for an entire lifetime.

Because the journey to faith involves several steps

This Because Approach guide, 'Innovating church for all,' is about innovating contextually appropriate ministries that tackle the barriers people face to progressing on the journey of faith. When we can identify particular barriers people face in our setting, it will be easier to develop effective ways of demolishing them. When we develop ministries that target the needs at a particular stage of the journey of faith it is also easier to link together ministries at each stage into an overall strategic process:

It's unrealistic to think that many people will turn up at a church service or course until Christians have befriended and invited them. It's also pointless to invite people to an event that explains Christian faith before they are willing to listen.

The Because Approach guide, 'Innovating church for all,' starts at the very beginning. It looks at ways of making the church accessible to all, including those:
– Who have no connection to the church
– Who have no interest in church
– Who harbour hostility towards the church.

Stages of the journey

Relationship building.	Respect building.	Relevance building.	Response building.

This Because Approach guide, 'Innovating church for all,' identifies ways to engage with people not yet Christians at each of four key stages of the journey of faith:

First Stage: Building Relationships
– I know some Christians
(Step 2 of **Innovating church for all**)

Matthew 4:19
'Come, follow me,' Jesus said, 'and I will make you fishers of men.'

Second Stage: Building Respect
– I respect the Christians I know
(Step 3 of **Innovating church for all**)

Third Stage: Building Relevance
– I see the relevance of Christianity to life
(Step 4 of **Innovating church for all**)

Fourth Stage: Building Response
– I understand my need of Jesus as Lord
(Step 5 of **Innovating church for all**)

Barriers to progress on the journey

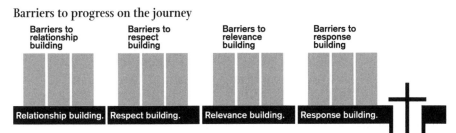

Barriers at the relationship building stage
– People live increasingly fluid and busy lives. As a result they become lonely and isolated, without many stable long-term relationships. In particular, there are many people who do not know any Christians as friends and have little idea what Christianity is about.

Barriers at the respect building stage
– Often people have a false impression of Christians shaped by various media. Christians are seen as slightly weird extremists or sad individuals who need a crutch to get through life. People don't see the impact faith has in daily action.

Barriers at the relevance building stage
– Many people reject Christianity by saying 'it's lovely that you've got your faith / religion but I don't need it / it's not my thing'. The challenge is to show people that Christ is more than 'their thing' – he's their King and relevant to life now and for eternity.

Barriers at the response building stage
– Some people hear and understand the message of the gospel but, like the rich man (Matt. 19:16-22), they walk away when they see the cost of commitment.

Solutions to the barriers

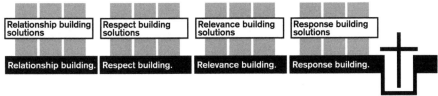

Relationship building solutions that help us make contact and form relationships
– Examples: social, sports, cultural events

Respect building solutions that demonstrate the goodness of God
– Examples: parent and toddler groups, community projects, youth clubs

Relevance building solutions that relate faith to life
– Examples: seeker-orientated services, topical courses, discussion groups

Response building solutions that show the truth of the gospel and the need to accept Jesus as Lord
– Examples: evangelistic courses, talks and one-to-one conversations

Because there are hindrances to strategy
(The 'strategy expertise' barrier to preparation)

Are we willing to co-operate with God's plans by living intentional lives? Several factors can prevent us from fulfilling God's specific plans for our church.

The skill shortage
Many churches have leaders who are intuitively strategic – they have no formal training but formulate visions and plans naturally. The rest of us, however, need training in how to discern, articulate and implement strategic plans.

So what?
The Because Approach provides a blank strategic framework ready to be filled in.

The confidence threat
Some churches don't have a strategic plan because they've lost confidence:
– In the irresistible power of the 'foolish' gospel
– In the redemptive potential of the local church as God's distribution channel of grace to the world.

So what?
The Because Approach aims to excite us afresh about the role Jesus gives his church. The website will enable churches to share stories of how biblical principles bring biblical fruit. (www. becauseapproach.com)

The turnkey mentality
Preparing a strategic plan involves taking a complete overview of current activities. It means taking a long, hard and honest look at your strengths, weaknesses, opportunities and threats. For some people, that prospect can seem too big a task and more than a little painful and threatening. Others may think that a strategic review is unnecessary and a distraction from getting on with the work. For these and other reasons, churches often opt for 'off-the-shelf' solutions. In the trade these are called 'turnkey' or 'plug and play' strategies because you plug them into your church, turn the key and let them play out their agenda. But there is a danger in thinking that 'one size fits all' in church. While every church has the same scriptural mandate from God, it also has a unique calling to carry out that mandate in their unique setting.

So what?
Ready-made programmes are useful as a starting point, but you will need to tailor them to your situation. Questions to ask include:
– What are its aims? It may be a great thing, but does it fit with the flow and logic of our strategy?
– What is the content? Is it in line with our theology?
– Are the materials clear and understandable for our audience?
– Is the 'feel' of the programme, in terms of its brand image and design, attractive to our audience?
If you answer 'no' to any of these questions, it may be necessary to amend the programme (if that is allowed under the copyright) or add extra elements to make it more culturally relevant and accessible. Alternatively, you will need to find another programme that fits with your situation.

The new big idea cycle
One major reason why churches often don't have a long-range strategic plan is that they frequently change direction. One of the keys to strategy is building momentum for a vision. Each time the vision changes, momentum is lost. This is a particular problem with

waves of fashion about 'the big new thing'. Churches are in danger of getting on the new idea bandwagons – Alpha one year, seeker services the next, cell church the year after, followed by planting, café church and the rest. But while all of these ideas may be great in particular contexts, they all take concentrated amounts of vision casting and encouraging – both of which are resources that don't replenish quickly. Once you've cast a vision for something new and poured your energy into getting it off the ground, there's a considerable time lag before you're ready to cast a vision for something different.

Churches also tend to change direction with the appointment of new leaders. The temptation for anyone coming into a church in a leadership position is to want to make their mark. But making your own mark often involves rubbing out the mark made before you arrived. In some cases this will be a good idea, but sometimes the foundation laid by someone else is a good one.

When you have agreed a clear and strategic plan, you can test new ideas against the plan. That way the plan sets the agenda and maintains the direction, rather than the new idea. In the same way, a new leader coming in can be seen to make a positive contribution to a plan already agreed.

The volunteer dilemma

The more church is seen as a leisure pursuit that people opt in or out of as they want to, the lower the level of commitment will be. A strategic plan resists the prevailing consumer mentality by casting a vision for the privileges of being part of God's kingdom-building team in a church.

The excess of choice

There are so many possible church activities but so little time. At any Christian conference these days you're presented with a mouth-watering menu of seminars, and when you walk into the resources tent you feel like a kid in a toyshop. 'I'll have half a dozen of these resource packs and I'll take a couple of those new ideas while I'm at it, and to be honest all these programmes look good so I'll buy one of each.' When endless products and programmes compete to help us with each ministry, how can we avoid idea overload?

So what?
Strategic tactics may change and plans will develop but a mission and vision owned by the whole church will be the long-term underpinning of a strategy.

So what?
Strategic plans are only of value in mobilising volunteers when the vision running through all activities is clearly communicated and is compelling enough to be a part of.

So what?
Step 6 of The Because Approach gives the opportunity to cut down a long 'wish list' of ideas to a focused, coherent and achievable set of ministry plans.

Because strategy is a partnership with the God of growth
(The 'strategy process' barrier to preparation)

When I started as Vicar at St James Clerkenwell we
had a launch service. The bishop did the legal bits and
preached, but he allowed me to give a presentation on
my plans for the church. I'd only just moved into the area
two weeks before and wasn't starting the job until the
next day, but in my extreme arrogance and naiveté I still
thought I knew what was what.

I announced that we were going to have three Sunday
services and three midweek activities (in addition to
existing Scouts, Guides, etc.):
– TGI-Sunday: a fun-filled, seeker-friendly service for all
ages with a film studio theme in which we would make a
video of a Bible story
– JC-Word: a classic morning service with relevant Bible
teaching for the people of Clerkenwell
– JC-Access: an evening service in the informal setting of
our crypt in which we could discuss the passage from the
morning and dig deeper
– JC-PowerPoint: a weekly gathering for prayer and
fellowship as a church
– JC-Why: an evangelistic course
– Two by Two Club: a parent and toddler group

The reality, however, turned out to be rather different.
People didn't go to the services they were 'meant to' go to!
– TGI-Sunday was designed for families from the estates,
but they came later to JC-Word.
– JC-Word was targeted especially for young professionals
in the loft apartments, but some preferred the high jinks
of TGI-Sunday.
– Students weren't meant to be out of bed till the
afternoon, but some opted to come in the morning
anyway.
– The Christians we assumed would transfer to us (who
were driving past us on the way to other big churches)
didn't.
– The people God sent to us didn't neatly fit the categories
we'd predetermined.

We saw very quickly that God wasn't calling us to be a copy of existing central London churches. Instead, we were to reach the people who had never heard of the big churches but knew of us because they lived near to us.
– To help clarify our particular role within the offering of London churches we used various mottos as a form of shorthand summary of what we were about. Examples included, 'church for those not used to church' and 'reaching the people other churches cannot reach' (based on the strap line for a well known beer that 'refreshes the parts other beers cannot reach')
– To help communicate our particular vision of being a church starting with people a long way back who first needed to develop an interest in Christian things as well as being a church looking to attain to the whole measure of the fullness of Christ (Eph. 4:13) we decided on the mission statement 'to build a thirst for God's rescue and a devotion to God rule'.

We also saw that people wanted services to be relevant and professional, but they didn't want them to be too focused on their specific interest group. In fact, one of the things people loved was meeting other locals, completely different from themselves, who they wouldn't otherwise meet. So, within a year, we'd changed to one service on a Sunday which had TGI-Sunday action, JC-Word relevance and the informal community of JC-Access. The unifying vision was that every Sunday would be consciously geared to meet the needs of people with no experience of church.

The process of adjusting our plans was ongoing. So, as we grew, we introduced a small group element to our weekly gatherings all together and then began to meet in homes on alternate weeks. We continued to change the structure of our Sunday service on a regular basis. We also continued to introduce 'one-off' events and new ideas to keep the church fresh and adaptable.

In all of this we learned that planning is useful but, when you're in partnership with Jesus, he takes your best-laid plans and makes them into something better than you dare imagine!

Solutions for churches

1. Analyse your current situation

A. SWOT analysis
When beginning strategic planning it's important to know the point you're starting from so you know how far you need to go to get to the place you decide to head for.

The 'industry standard' method of analysing the current situation is the 'SWOT' analysis.
Strengths:
– What aspects of your church are going well?
– What are you able to do effectively as a church because of the situation God has called you into?

Weaknesses:
– What limits your effectiveness in what you do and who you are as a church?

Opportunities:
– What are the benefits of being in your particular situation as a church?

Threats:
– What is hampering your hopes and dreams as a church?

Strengths	Weaknesses
Opportunities	Threats

B. Gap analysis
The Because Approach puts the four key stages on the journey to faith into a four step process. As each step is described, many ideas and solutions will be discussed. It is useful therefore to know your starting point as a church in terms of current activities that fit each stage, activities that do not fit and gaps where there are no activities at present. Knowing where you are starting from will help focus your discussion at each stage and give the encouragement that you're developing what's already good rather than starting from scratch all the time.

List current activities under the headings:

step 2: Relationship building activities

step 3: Respect building activities

step 4: Relevance building activities

step 5: Response building activities

– Where do you already have enough activities?
– Where are the gaps?
– What activities don't fit into any stage? Why? Are they necessary to keep?

Solutions for churches

2. Review your mission statement

The scriptural 'because' of your church will be summed up in an overall mission statement as well as a set of biblical values. A mission statement answers the question 'why do we exist' and values answer the question 'what beliefs compel us'. The biblical values relating to the church's evangelistic task of making disciples (innovating church for all) will be clarified at each step of the Because Approach (see study guides 2-5 and summary in study guide 6).

But before beginning this process it is important to review and confirm your overall aim. Mission statements are fixed as the overarching long-term goal against which all strategies and activities are measured. Do you have as a starting point to the Because Approach a memorable mission statement that sums up the calling of your church?

All mission statements have at their core the same timeless biblical mission of the church to make and grow disciples – or, as it's often put, 'to know Christ and to make him known'.

The wording of the mission statement will reflect the character and context of a particular church:
– Some reflect geographic position (e.g. 'to win and hold the centre of a world capital for Christ' emphasizes the role of this church within a city)
– Some reflect strategic emphasis (e.g. 'to build a thirst for God's rescue and devotion to God's rule' emphasizes the strategy of starting further back with people who have little interest in Christianity)
– Some reflect particular theological emphases (e.g. growing upwards – towards God; growing inwards – within the church family; growing outwards – to the local community)
– Some reflect a desire for brevity (e.g. 'bring in, build up, send out')

3. Agree to commit your plans to God in prayer

As we've seen, planning is co-operating with God and discerning his purposes. For that reason we need to ask for God's spiritual wisdom and understanding, God's eyes of compassion for people, God's eternal priorities. We also need to be willing at every stage to 'go with' the new opportunities God gives rather than being restricted to a fixed long-range plan which may not be what God has in mind.

Study Guide 1.

Discussion starter
What makes your church different from a social club?

SCRIPTURE
SETTING
SOLUTION
3

Study Scripture 1 Corinthians 7:17–24
What does Paul say our attitude should be to our current situation?

Study Scripture Matthew 28:16–20
What is the church's reason for being?

Apply: What is your church doing to fulfil this mandate? Are there things that you should be doing? Are there things that you could stop doing?

Study Scripture Zechariah 4:1–8
God says don't rely on 'physical ability or military might'[3] (v. 6) when facing opposition (the mighty mountain of v. 7). In what ways are we drawn away from relying on God?

Apply: How can we ensure that reliance on God is at the heart of our plans?

Study Scripture Nehemiah 1
What is the content and purpose of Nehemiah's prayer?
Why is prayer the first and foremost activity of any strategic planning process?

Preparation.

SCRIPTURE

SETTING 3

SOLUTION

Analyse your setting
What is your church's current situation?
Identify who you are, who you know and what you do as a
church under the 'SWOT' headings (See solutions page 30)

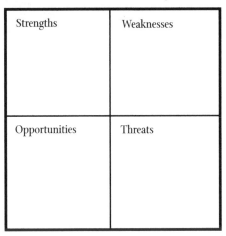

Strengths	Weaknesses
Opportunities	Threats

Analyse your setting
What is your attitude to the situation you've just identified?
In the light of 1 Corinthians 7:17–24, what should your attitude be? It may be far from
perfect, but in what ways can you see your situation as a calling to remain within?

Analyse your setting
List your current outreach activities under the 4 stages of Relationship, Respect, Relevance
and Response building. Where do you already have enough activities? Where are the gaps?
What areas should be a focus for development? Which items don't fit anywhere and why?

Relationship building.

Respect building.

Relevance building.

Response building.

Preparation solutions.

Discuss and decide solutions

Do you have a memorable mission statement that sums up the calling of your church?

Does it reflect the twin purposes of making and growing disciples?

Does its phrasing reflect the character and context of your particular church?

In the light of your discussion so far, does your mission statement need to be rewritten?

Discuss and decide solutions

Ideas for prayer feature in every 'solutions' section of the Because Approach. But how will you make prayer the powerhouse of your planning process, as it was for Nehemiah?

[1] *Jerry Maguire* (Columbia/TriStar Pictures, 1996; video distribution: Sony Music Operations).

[2] *Gladiator* (Dreamworks Pictures and Universal Pictures, 2000; video distribution: Columbia/Tristar Home Video, UK).

[3] *Simon Birch* (Hollywood Pictures, 1999; video distribution: Buena Vista Home Entertainment Ltd.).

[4] Ralph L. Smith, *Micah – Malachi* (Word Biblical Commentary; Waco, TX: Word, 1984).

Matthew 9:37-38
Then [Jesus] said to his disciples,
'The harvest is plentiful but the workers are few.
Ask the Lord of the harvest, therefore,
to send out workers into his harvest field.'

Relationship building.

'Because churches are called to go.'

When I was a student I signed up to join the parachute club. It seemed like a good way of meeting people without having to run up and down a cold, wet length of grass. All parachuting meant was getting a lift to the top and then hanging there whilst you came back down. At first, the club weekend away seemed just the ticket. We had a series of lectures on technique and safety in a nice warm hut off the airstrip. Even the practice jumps were inside a hangar, and we spent lots of time in the café on the airbase, drinking hot coffee and eating warm pies – I loved it! But then it came time to get in the plane and be taken up into the sky. Once in the air, I waited in line with sweaty palms and second thoughts. But there was no turning back, and when the green light came on indicating that I was to leave the plane there was only one thing left for the instructor to say: 'Go!'

With similar urgency, Jesus trained his followers and modelled that Christians are to 'Go!' Almost the first thing Jesus says to Simon Peter and Andrew is that following him will involve going fishing for people (Matt. 4:19). Right from the start Jesus took his disciples 'people-fishing' (Matt. 4:23). The last thing Jesus says to his disciples is on exactly the same theme – go and make disciples of all nations (Matt. 28:19). In effect Jesus says to his church, 'I've taught you what to do – now go and do it.'

Church growth isn't just a matter of keeping birth rates higher than death rates. Nor will the church of God grow as individuals switch from one congregation to another. Growing churches are those involved in reaching out to prospective new members – and that will mean starting with activities deliberately aimed at meeting them and building relationships with them.

It's a lot more comfortable staying inside with people you know, but unless we're going churches we'll never be growing churches. We may be nervous when Jesus gives us the green light and the only thing left to do is 'Go!' But when we do go, we know that surely Jesus is with us to the end of the age.

Because God's heart is for people

We've probably all heard children being taught this theology of the church: 'Here's the church, here's the steeple. Open the door and...' Stop! No, the people are not the fingers inside the church. The people are the church!

When our Sunday service is finished and I lock the door and set the alarm, I don't leave the church – it has already left! Any phrase that implies the church is about buildings or programmes or staff teams is dangerous, because it devalues the role of the people. Such thinking makes people into the raw material that churches process, or the customers that churches sell to, or the output that churches fashion. To borrow and change a phrase from the presidential campaign of George Bush Senior: 'it's all about the people, stupid!'

People are God's first priority throughout the Bible. God makes only people in his own image. God places people in the garden and gives them his authority to rule. Only people are given the ability to relate to God in a personal way. Even after the first two people rejected God, the Creator's heart for people continued. He provided clothes for Adam and Eve and promised a way back to him. Rather than leave them to live forever in broken relationship, God planned the day when the destroyer serpent would be crushed and people would be restored in relationship with him.

That's God's heart – the constant refrain of the Bible is 'I will be their God, and they will be my people'. God is a God of his people and with his people – not God in a building that his people visit once a week if he's lucky! God promises Abraham a people as numerous as the stars, and God promises David that the dynasty of people will be eternal. At the beginning of his ministry, Jesus points to that promise to David when he declares that 'the kingdom of God is near'.

Genesis 1
26 Then God said, 'Let us make man in our image, in our likeness, and let them rule over the fish of the sea and the birds of the air, over the livestock, over all the earth, and over all the creatures that move along the ground.'

Genesis 17
8 'The whole land of Canaan, where you are now an alien, I will give as an everlasting possession to you and your descendants after you; and I will be their God.'

Genesis 26
4 'I will make your descendants as numerous as the stars in the sky and will give them all these lands, and through your offspring all nations on earth will be blessed'.

2 Samuel 7
11 'The LORD declares to you that the LORD himself will establish a house for you'.

16 'Your house and your kingdom shall endure for ever before me; your throne shall be established for ever.'

I met Raj when he came along to an evangelistic course at the church where I was a curate. Raj wanted his baby baptized and had accepted the invitation to come to the course with all the questions his incisive lawyer's mind could muster. During the course weekend Raj read a book about becoming a Christian and went off on his own and prayed a prayer of commitment to Christ. Nothing dramatic happened. But when I saw him Monday evening he told me how the most amazing thing had happened to him on the way to work. Walking down the hill to the station as he always did, he started thinking about the people in the cars passing him. He wondered who they were and how they felt. When he reached the station he started wondering the same about the ticket collector. Does he live around here? Does he have children? Does he know about Jesus? Tough Raj from the City was beginning to see people as Jesus saw them – they matter.

Jesus is serving notice to everyone that he has come to invite people to enter the eternal kingdom – God's 'new society'[1] of people who are devoted to Christ as their Saviour and Lord.

In John's Gospel, Jesus' first activities involve him socializing. In John 1:29 Jesus heads towards John the Baptist who was at Bethany, on the other side of the Jordan. It's not likely that Jesus just happened to be taking a riverside walk and bumped into John's baptism service. Jesus deliberately goes to meet him. John 1:40 tells us that he spent the whole day getting to know two of John's disciples, finding out all about them and building friendships with them. John 2 describes Jesus at a wedding reception. Throughout all four Gospels we encounter Jesus in people's homes, sharing life with them over meals. He was well known for this and was even criticized for being careless about the company he kept (Mark 2:16). Jesus liked being with people and went out of his way to meet new people in each village.

In fact, Jesus has a people-centred mission statement: Jesus replied, 'Let us go somewhere else – to the nearby villages – so that I can preach there also. That is why I have come.' (Mark 1:38)

Why did Jesus come?
To tell people that he can rescue them.

'For even the Son of Man did not come to be served, but to serve, and to give his life as a ransom for many.' (Mark 10:45)

Why did Jesus come?
To serve people by dying for them.

Because Jesus teaches us to make people our priority

The New Testament church started small, but its numbers quickly multiplied as the people continued, with the Spirit's power, to do what they'd seen Jesus do. Jesus had gone from village to village preaching about the kingdom of God and they did likewise, going gradually to all nations. Convinced of the importance of proclaiming the good news of God's kingdom, they followed Jesus' kingdom-extending plan. For example, in Matthew 10 Jesus says to the 12 disciples:

1. Go with my authority (v. 1)

Jesus gives his disciples authority to extend the kingdom of people devoted to God by giving them authority to demonstrate the life-changing work of God.

2. Go where I send you (v. 5)

At first glance this seems a bit narrow and unfair – but we know from Acts 1 that Jesus isn't anti-Samaritan or anti-Gentile. Before his ascension to heaven, the last thing Jesus says is:

'But you will receive power when the Holy Spirit comes on you; and you will be my witnesses in Jerusalem, and in all Judea and Samaria, and to the ends of the earth' (Acts 1:8).

Jesus wants us to go to all nations (Matt. 28:19). In this sense the command is universal, but he is specific about the people he wants us to invite to join his kingdom.

That's the second amazing truth for us – we've all been given a specific commission. Mine is to my neighbours in my street, friends I've met though my children's school, people who sit with me on the church steps at lunchtime, people who contact the church and people I've known in previous days of work and study.

But Jesus has not said, 'go into the offices of Morgan Stanley and establish my kingdom there' – that's Katherine's commission. Nor has he said, 'go into the depot of the number 4 bus and tell them about my rule' – that's George's commission. Where is your commission?

Matthew 10

1 He called his twelve disciples to him and gave them authority to drive out evil spirits and to heal every disease and sickness.
2 These are the names of the twelve apostles: first, Simon (who is called Peter) and his brother Andrew; James son of Zebedee, and his brother John; 3 Philip and Bartholomew; Thomas and Matthew the tax collector; James son of Alphaeus, and Thaddaeus; 4 Simon the Zealot and Judas Iscariot, who betrayed him.
5 These twelve Jesus sent out with the following instructions: 'Do not go among the Gentiles or enter any town of the Samaritans. 6 Go rather to the lost sheep of Israel. 7 As you go, preach this message: "The kingdom of heaven is near." 8 Heal the sick, raise the dead, cleanse those who have leprosy, drive out demons. Freely you have received, freely give. 9 Do not take along any gold or silver or copper in your belts; 10 take no bag for the journey, or extra tunic, or sandals or a staff; for the worker is worth his keep.
11 Whatever town or village you enter, search for some worthy person there and stay at his house until you leave. 12 As you enter the home, give it your greeting. 13 If the home is deserving, let your peace rest on it; if it is not, let your peace return to you. 14 If anyone will not welcome you or listen to your words, shake the dust off your feet when you leave that home or town.

'There is church because there is mission, not vice versa.'[2]

3. Go to lost people (v. 6)
The work of extending God's kingdom is urgent and vital. Jesus tells us to go to people who are spiritually lost, cut off from a relationship with God.

4. Go with my message (v. 7)
The message of the kingdom is of life-and-death importance:
– It's the life-saving message of restored relationship with God
– It's the life-giving message of access into God's family
– It's the life-sustaining message of the new earth which is to come.

5. Go to receptive people (v. 11)
Jesus' instruction to his followers is very simple: look for the 'worthy person' or 'man of peace' (Luke 10:6) and stay with that person. In other words, if you're going to have influence in a village you need to start small, with one household, but spend your time wisely with a sympathetic household who will listen rather than 'casting pearls before swine'. Jesus is clear that many will reject the message, so we shouldn't be surprised by or waste time with fruitless relationships – shrewdness and innocence are qualities to pray for (v. 16).

Acts 16
13 On the Sabbath we went outside the city gate to the river, where we expected to find a place of prayer. We sat down and began to speak to the women who had gathered there. 14 One of those listening was a woman named Lydia, a dealer in purple cloth from the city of Thyatira, who was a worshipper of God. The Lord opened her heart to respond to Paul's message.

The church grew as gospel people met other people who in time also became gospel people.

Paul followed Jesus' model when he arrived in Philippi. He didn't just stand on a soapbox in the town square, shout his piece and then catch the last train out of there. He waited till the Sabbath to meet people. He knew that Philippi had very few Jews and no synagogue, and he did further research to find out where the people went to pray – by the river just outside the city walls. When he went there, he sought out the 'worthy person' or 'person of peace' (Matt. 10:11). All of this is people-centred (and time-consuming). But consider the results...

Lydia, a Gentile businesswoman, responded to Paul's explanation of the gospel. But Paul didn't just add her to his list of converts and move on. He spent time with her, prepared her for baptism and stayed with her family for a time. In fact, we learn in verse 40 that the First Philippi Community Church met initially in her home.

Because we need to be reminded to make people our priority

The apostle Paul is clear that his mission is to people – and not just to people like himself. He tells the Corinthians (1 Cor. 9:19–22) that he is so committed to people, he is willing to become like them in order to have a greater opportunity to save them. Paul's examples demonstrate how uncomfortable it can be to put people first – prioritizing people meant making himself a slave to people and engaging with the world in which they lived. Yet Paul was willing to employ all possible means and become all things in his bid to help all the people he could to pass from death to life.

Are people that much of a priority for us? Are we willing to become slaves to people not like us in order to bring them to life with us in eternity? That's the question the people of God faced when they were exiled from Israel to Babylon. At first just the 10,000 leaders were sent into exile, and the prophet Hananiah persuaded them not to mix with the Babylonians. He wanted everyone to live outside the city to keep themselves separate and pure. But the prophet Jeremiah heard about this and wrote them a letter from Jerusalem, correcting Hananiah's error. Jeremiah gives God's clear and surprising instruction: go into Babylon, live in Babylon, get involved in the lives of the Babylonians and influence the culture of the Babylonians. But going takes guts – it's much easier to be a holy huddle. Becoming a Babylonian in order to save some will take us out of our comfort zone. That's why we need encouragement to go for it.

We need to remember the words of 'the other Lord's prayer'[3] in Matthew 9:38. Jesus doesn't doubt that there's a full harvest of people open to the gospel. He doesn't tell us to pray for opportunities as much as for willing workers who will follow the call and go. It's a prayer we can ask, but also a prayer that may involve us as the answer. Jesus gives four reasons for taking up his call to go:

1 Corinthians 9
19 Though I am free and belong to no man, I make myself a slave to everyone, to win as many as possible.

22 To the weak I became weak, to win the weak. I have become all things to all men so that by all possible means I might save some.

Jeremiah 29
4 This is what the LORD Almighty, the God of Israel, says to all those I carried into exile from Jerusalem to Babylon: 5 'Build houses and settle down; plant gardens and eat what they produce. 6 Marry and have sons and daughters; find wives for your sons and give your daughters in marriage, so that they too may have sons and daughters. Increase in number there; do not decrease. 7 Also, seek the peace and prosperity of the city to which I have carried you into exile. Pray to the LORD for it, because if it prospers, you too will prosper.'

Matthew 9
35 Jesus went through all the towns and villages, teaching in their synagogues, preaching the good news of the kingdom and healing every disease and sickness. 36 When he saw the crowds, he had compassion on them, because they were harassed and helpless, like sheep without a shepherd. 37 Then he said to his disciples, 'The harvest is plentiful but the workers are few. 38 Ask the Lord of the harvest, therefore, to send out workers into his harvest field.'

When you buy a coffee at Starbucks you have a choice – you can have your latte in a china mug to drink on the premises or you can have it in a paper cup to go.

You don't get that choice at church. The spiritual drink that's poured out during our hour and a bit together on a Sunday isn't to be consumed then and there to give a warm fuzzy feeling and a spiritual caffeine kick. The messages we hear from the Bible are 'to go'. When you're reminded of God's goodness at church, go and tell others. When you're convicted of God's authority at church, go and serve him as your authority. When you drink at the well of God's love and grace, go and pour that love and grace into the lives of others.

'The story of the young church, and the dynamics by which it came to birth, bear witness to a church born to reproduce; not just planting churches but with an ecclesiological instinct for furthering God's mission.'[5]

1. Jesus is not asking us to do anything he didn't do himself – he has shown us how and demonstrated that it is possible (v. 35).

2. We go out of compassion for people who are harassed and people who will remain helpless unless we, or someone else, introduce them to the Good Shepherd. Since we know the solution to their need, it would be incredibly unloving not to go and share it (v. 36).

3. The hard work has been done already. The harvest isn't the problem – as we have seen, it's the workers Jesus tells us to pray for. There isn't a crop shortage, because crop growth is God's department and he never fails to deliver. The weak link in the chain is the willingness of people to do the much simpler job of going into the Son-ripened fields (v. 37).

4. The harvest field belongs to God, and he will call people to go to his fields when we ask him to (v. 38). So what are we waiting for? Our Master says to us, 'Go from village to village, go and make disciples, go into all nations. Don't just sit there – the green light is on, the harvest fields are full – go!'

The apostle Paul followed his Master's command and thus began the strategic work of planting reproducible churches. Paul demonstrates that priority in Romans 15 when he says, 'from Jerusalem all the way round to Illyricum, I have fully proclaimed the gospel of Christ' (v. 19), and 'there is no more place for me to work in these regions' (v. 23). As Leslie Newbigin points out, 'What, exactly, has Paul done? Certainly not converted all the populations of those regions. Certainly not solved their social and economic problems. He has in his own words "fully preached the gospel" and left behind communities of men and women who believe the gospel and live by it.'[4]

Making people our priority will mean going like missionaries into cultural sub-groups within our networks where Christ is not known and planting gospel communities.

Because people are increasingly isolated
(The 'isolated' barrier to relationship building)

There is a great sense of isolation and fragmentation in society.[6]

1. Because more people live alone
In the three decades from 1971 to 2003:
– The proportion of the UK adult population living alone has more than doubled
– The percentage of single parents in the UK adult population tripled.

2. Because fewer people remain committed to marriage:
– The number of couples marrying at all has dropped sharply
– People are waiting longer before getting married or cohabiting first
– The average age of people marrying for the first time in is rising
– The number of marriages ending in divorce has doubled in 30 years.

3. Because people have less time to socialize
The amount of time people spend sleeping and doing essential tasks has remained the same over the last 10 years, but work now takes a greater share of the hours in the day – leaving less time for leisure activities. The average number of hours per week spent at work was 37.3 in 1991, and 42 in 2002.
An increasing number of workers, in the words of one psychotherapist, are 'type-A dynamite kegs' prone to heart attacks, high blood pressure and migraines who find that 'their work schedules are getting in the way of their enjoyment of life'.

4. Because people move house more frequently
A global economy and concentration of employment in increasingly multinational companies mean that people move locations with their jobs more frequently.

All of these factors hamper the formation of consistent long-term relationships. A *Friends* TV-show-style community of friends who live near each other and meet frequently in each other's homes and the coffee shop may be a great concept, but it is not common. Building deep community takes a huge amount of time and effort and is not helped by the hassles of travel (not everyone can live in central Manhattan) and the demands of work. Such community can also unravel quickly when members of the group relocate or relationships break down. The busier work gets, the more demands family life makes, the more times relationships go bad, the more times relocation means building relationships from scratch again – the easier it is to stay home alone with the TV.

This view of church as a distinctive community for all is increasingly challenged. Pete Ward, for example, writes:

'The nostalgic community sells itself as the one place where communal meetings remain possible in society. We tell ourselves that in church young and old gather together in ways they never do outside of church. This kind of myth makes us feel good about our congregation. The nostalgic community of church is more wish fulfilment than reality.'[8]

But should we not aim to make the wishes of Christ in Scripture reality? Isn't church a taste of heaven on earth? It may be that our evangelistic groups are geared to specific cultures, and even our small groups may gather with a particular cultural or interest focus. But our public meetings should be precisely that – gatherings where all sections of the public are welcome, included and challenged with the universally relevant gospel.

My experience is that unbelievers love the fact that they meet a wide range of local people when they come to St James on a Sunday morning, and they would resist being forced into a mono-cultural gathering and treated like processed peas.

Just as the BBC offers programmes that are of interest to a wide spectrum of the population as well as specialist programmes for a narrower audience, church needs to have entry point gatherings for a wide range of contemporary people as well as more specialized activities to meet specific needs.

So what?

A church in any context has a great opportunity to be a place where anyone can experience a community with roots that go back many thousands of years, a community that doesn't have entry requirements or a probationary period, a community where everyone is included – not just as a group of friends in a coffee shop, but as a family belonging to God.

The challenge is to encourage existing members to have a 'recruiting mindset', always looking for opportunities to invite non-members to become part of God's eternal community.

There may be a general willingness to consider inviting people to church events, but in reality not much more than a third of churchgoers have done so in the last 12 months.

When 100,000 English churchgoers were asked 'would you be prepared to invite to a church service here any of your friends and relatives who do not currently attend a church?'[7] they replied:

'No, definitely not'	1%
'No, probably not'	9%
'Yes, but haven't in the last 12 months'	42%
'Yes, and have in the last 12 months'	38%
'Don't know'	10%

Experiencing community where people share not only the gospel, but their lives as well, is highly attractive.

There are only three buildings in Clerkenwell where you can go and be guaranteed to meet every type of local resident: the supermarket, the tube station and the local church. The church is the only one of those three where you're likely to experience decent conversation (unless you enjoy arguments fuelled by trolley rage!).

The pubs, bars and restaurants in our local area are remarkably segregated – all catering to a certain type of clientele. But the church building is a public house of God – where God's people welcome every member of the community and offer each one the refreshment of life in relationship with God and his earthly family.

Because church is not located where people are located
(The 'liquid' barrier to relationship building)

The concepts of 'a job for life', living in 'a house for life' and going to 'a church for life' no longer exist in our fluid culture. The church's mission to go into a liquid world and make disciples presents three major challenges:

1. Liquid society
In a global village where travel is fast and communication is increasingly electronic, people don't necessarily have a strong affinity to a geographic area but see their location in terms of a number of overlapping networks of relationships.

So what?
Some people are drawn to a church by the people in their network who go, not by where on the map it gathers – for them affinity is key, not location. The challenge for a church built around an affinity group is to include in the body those who aren't to type. The unity of community is the biblical antidote to liquid individualism. Church should be a place where you fit in even if you don't fit the mould.

2. Liquid missiology
Contextualization is not the exclusive preserve of missionaries abroad. Local churches in every situation need to become that situation – in a liquid society 'I become liquid to save some'.

So what?
All activities that churches plan need to fit with the way people are, as well as with what they need. In fact, before we will have the opportunity to show the relevance of Christianity to an unbeliever's world (step 4, 'Relevance Building', in the Because Approach), we need to inhabit their world with them and build a relational bridge to them.

'Modernity is undergoing a liquifying process... Changes in productive processes mean that individuals can no longer expect to follow a safe career within one organisation... A flexible workforce is made up of individual consumers who find their identity in how they live rather than social class... The individual has to shape identity apart from community.'[9]

'People do not build their meaning in local societies... they select their relationships on the basis of their affinities' (Manuel Castells).[10]

'A faithful Church is continually shaped by its inner dynamic: the flow of Apostolic Tradition, with Scripture as its norm... The Church is, however, also shaped by the kind of world in which it finds itself. This must mean a constant receiving of the Gospel into our particular context' (Michael Nazir-Ali).[11]

'The church must always be willing to die to its own cultural comfort in order to live where God intends it to be. "One size fits all" won't do. No one expression or shape of church life will fit our diverse consumer culture' (Graham Cray).[12]

'When so called "traditional" churches are out of touch with the people who live around them, the problem is not that they are irrelevant, but that they are not incarnational' (Tex Sample).[13]

'A missional church seeks to discern God's specific missional vocation for the entire community and all its members. The issue of cultural context is essential because the missional church shapes itself to fit that context in order to transform it for the sake of the Kingdom.'[15]

'It is no longer possible for us to think in terms of bringing people back to Christ or even back to the church. They have never yet been in order to have left... It is pointless trying to encourage yet more effective "come" structures when what is called for is to develop "go" structures in which the church learns afresh how to be missionaries in our own land. The planting of new missionary congregations represents a vital ingredient in developing these new "go" structures.'[16]

'We do not need to choose between "go" and "come"; both are valid forms of evangelism. Some people will be reached by attraction, while others will be reached by confrontation. A balanced, healthy church should provide opportunities and programs for both. At Saddleback, we use both approaches. We say "Come and see!" to our community, but to our core we say, "Go and tell!"'[17]

'The life of any church is only as long as it reproduces itself. The local church is always one generation from extinction. And we can no longer presume upon an automatic ability to reproduce ourselves, because the pool of people who regard church as relevant is decreasing with every generation.'[18]

3. Liquid ecclesiology?

Dr David Barrett[14] talks about the rise of the so-called 'neo-apostolics' who, he says:
– 'Reject historical denominationalism and restrictive overbearing central authority'
– 'Seek a more effective missionary lifestyle'.
Alan Hirsch, an advocate of this church movement talks about the 'missional incarnational impulse' of 'seeding an incarnational work' where the ecclesiology of the church follows as the church takes shape within its context.

So what?

Rather than saying to people, 'Come to us and do church our way', we need to be going to people and working out what it might mean to apply the scriptural principles of church to their situation. It's exciting to see how Scripture directs us to establish solid cross-boundary communities in a world of liquid individualism. In effect, church is the opposite of a soft-centre chocolate – church has a solid centre of community but a more liquid outside which is accessible to all people and adaptable to different people.

The call for churches to be incarnational in their communities has helpfully re-emphasized the need for churches to be going into the world rather than just assuming people will come to them. But there's no need to set up a false dichotomy between a 'go' and 'come' strategy. Often, like the woman at the well, we go to people in order to say 'Come, see a man who told me everything I ever did. Could this be the Christ?' (John 4:29). And even if we do all of our evangelism one-to-one in people's homes, we're still at some point going to want them to come and gather with other Christians. After all, 'church' is simply the biblical word for a gathering of Christians – whether that gathering has grown out of a community project or meets in an ecclesiastical building.

Fresh expressions of church and missionary congregations are still gatherings of people by definition even though they may be very different gatherings in application. Building church for all will involve having a come and go strategy. In the parable of the great banquet, we're to go out in order to invite people to come in (Luke 14:23).

Because church is not the only gathering of people
(The 'multi choice' barrier to relationship building)

Long gone are the days when the only thing to do on a Sunday morning was go to church. Church is one of many options available to the modern consumer – all competing to offer a sense of community, friendship, value and acceptance. People have such leveraged diaries, with multiple activities scheduled in every hour of every day, that the concept of a day of rest gets lost in a whirl of poly-phasing plate spinning!

1. There are many alternatives to church
One Surrey church, for example, has found that:
– Saturday evening is the social night – dinner parties, etc.
– Sunday morning is for hockey, athletics, football and rugby
– Sunday afternoon is for cricket
– Sunday evening is for homework.

2. Consumer choice is king
Nick Spencer, a trends and attitudes analyst with The London Institute for Contemporary Christianity, conducted group interviews with a range of people from the 66% of the population who are neither convinced atheists nor definite believers in God.[21] He found that, when asked how churches should address future challenges, respondents focused on consumerist principles:
'I think there should be large sitting rooms...and coffee.'
'If it was a bit more social... It's got to be more entertaining.'

3. Alternatives to church can grow in appeal
At the end of the 1990s a major survey was published on why people stopped going to church. Gone but not Forgotten[22] reached the surprising conclusion that people didn't leave churches so much because of loss of faith as they did because of loss of interest. The survey asked respondents to look at a battery of 168 questions and identify those which best described why they had been attending church less frequently. Seventy-one per cent said they simply 'got out of the habit of going to church'.

'The dilemma for families is that the children have to choose between pleasing their parents by going to church or pursuing their sport.'[19]

The Gone but not Forgotten survey also highlighted how often changes in lifestyle – such as going to college or a new job or moving house – can be catalysts for people giving up on attending church. In today's multinational and merger-driven economy people are increasingly mobile.

But with each relocation or step up the property ladder, church involvement tends to slip down the list of priorities.

Why?
– Some simply get out of the habit with the new routines of a new place.
– Some continue to hanker after their old church and don't find a local church that matches up.
– Some lack the enthusiasm to invest the same levels of energy in a new community and decide to take a break from being so involved.
– Some find it hard, as a 'new kid on the block' rather than a core team member, to break into a church of existing relationships and ministries.

'One mum in her thirties said to me, "Chobham Rugby Club is my church." That's where people go each week and that's where they get their friendship and sense of coming together. I experienced that when I enquired about my children joining a rugby club. Someone sent me an email straight away saying I was welcome to come down any week I wanted to and see if I liked it. The email ended "welcome on board". It was accepting, warm and didn't ask any searching questions about my kids' ability or whatever.'[20]

'People are reflexive because they continually review their sense of self in relation to the increasing number of choices available in society. The fact that there are many choices leads to a certain amount of insecurity... People face life's challenges and problems on their own.'[24]

So what?

1. Convenient meetings

Rather than arrogantly continue as we always have and demand that people fit round us, we need to look thoroughly at when, where and how we should be gathering as church. Is Sunday the best day? If so, what time is best? Is a church building the best place to meet or should we be meeting in homes, or a neutral venue which is familiar to people and easy to get to?

2. 'Customer support'

Growing companies have to balance various demands. Keeping existing customers requires customer support, while gaining new customers requires marketing. A growing church needs to maintain that same sort of balance. This can be particularly difficult in a setting where gaining new members is a lot harder than serving and keeping existing ones. Churches need to convince new 'customers' to commit some of their precious time and energy to the church community. But the commitment doesn't end there. Church members also need to help new members through the initial process of 'assimilation' into the church family.

3. Genuine community

One challenge is for churches to offer a welcome based on genuine biblical community and culturally appropriate community rather than consumer marketing techniques. As Simon Jones points out, 'superficial words of greeting from the front and the odd smile as you pass a visitor do not constitute a welcome'.[23] The question is, what does?

4. Customisation

'Mass customisation is advancing so rapidly that it is about to become the defining feature of our consumer world... We are moving from an off-the-peg to a tailor-made world... Post-modern values include the rejection of hierarchy, suspicion of institutions and strong emphasis on personal choice... By and large, the church is still stuck in the standardised world. It approaches evangelism with a mass mindset. "Come and join our church" is the invitation, which assumes that "our church" is suitable for the people we invite. "We like it so other people will." That is typical one-size-fits-all thinking.'[25]

Solutions research

COMMUTERS

HOPPERS

LOCALS
+
< 15 min walk
up to 20 min short hop by bus, car, bike etc.
> 20 min by bus, car, train etc.

There are three levels of proximity (the exact definitions for each will vary depending on your setting):

Locals – people who live or work within easy walking distance from the church (e.g., less than 15 minutes). They are likely to know where the church is even if they've never been in the building, and they probably pass nearby on a regular basis.

Hoppers – people who are within easy reach of the church by car or public transport. This will probably mean less than 20 or 25 minutes of travel time – they are close enough that the distance is not a barrier to coming to events on a regular basis.

Commuters (Network) – people who live further away from the church (e.g., more than 20 minutes) but would be willing to bear the cost of a longer commute because of the specific benefits the church is able to provide them or because the church has a particular focus on their network of friends.

1. Identify your current mix of local and network church.
Categorize existing members according to their proximity to the church.

2. Identify the main groups of people the church could reach.
For example, there may be distinct groups identifiable by types of housing, employment, level of proximity to the church (see above), cultural 'tribes' or friendship networks.

3. Gather data on each group.
a. Life stage
– left school but still in higher education, pre-job
– young (under 40) and single
– couples with no kids
– families with pre-school / primary school-age kids at home
– families with secondary school-age kids at home
– older (over 40) and single
– couples with kids who have left home
– retired
b. Economic environment
– Income
– Employment (also childcare availability and facilities for unemployed)
– Threat of crime
– Local economy (shops, facilities, etc.)
– Education (schools, colleges, training, etc.)
– Local issues (asylum, race, transport, etc.)
– Health issues (nutrition, stress, depression, substance abuse)
– Social issues (loneliness, suicide, divorce, disabilities)
c. Social life
– Where do people socialize?
– With whom do they socialize?
– What do they do when they socialize?

How?[26]

1. Visit the local library or local council for public data.
2. Buy data from market research firms.
3. Observe where people gather:
– Who's in the pubs, coffee bars, cinemas, restaurants, clubs? Who are they with, and how long do they stay?
– Who's in the parks, leisure centres, gyms and other recreation facilities? Who are they with, and how long do they stay?
4. Interview representative individuals or small groups.

Grouping people is a useful tool when developing strategies, but it's vital to remember that a church is all about people, not categories – a family of people with individual needs. As Douglas Coupland once put it, 'I'm not a target market.'

Example groupings[27] used by political market researchers:
(This is not an exhaustive list but rather illustrations to generate ideas for categorizing groupings in your setting.)

Cultural leaders
Educated people living in cities, many of whom work in the liberal professions, government or arts. Enjoy discussion of social issues over gourmet food.
Challenge to the church: eclectic taste in music which frowns on the middle-of-the-road modern music found in many churches. Value tolerance. Suspicious of religious certainty.

Success symbols
Professionals who work in the city for big firms. Travel a lot and have high disposable incomes. Have little time outside of exotic holidays. May prefer modern loft-style developments until their children are of school age.
Challenge to the church: Often away at the weekend at a second home. Less likely to see the need for church.

New kids on the block
Young professionals often living in rented city accommodation. Broadminded. Focused on establishing careers and having a good time.
Challenge for the church: Suspicious of power and institutions. Alienated by the music and culture of many churches. Move a lot so less likely to want a church that's local.

Upscaling new owners
Busy earning rather than consuming. Time is at a premium so want convenience.
Challenge to the church: Church unlikely to figure unless it can be accessed without too much effort and can be shown to contribute to the dream of a better life.

Affluent blue collar
Older manual workers settled in comfortable homes.
Challenge to the church: More likely to be seen in a shopping centre than a church on a Sunday.

High technologists
Live in large modern detached houses. Work for high-tech firms and use technology to the full in how they live, what they own, how they travel and what they do for entertainment.
Challenge to the church: May see the style of church as out of date and the message of church as out of touch with their modern lifestyle.

Towers and terraces
Live in estates and other terrace housing owned (or previously owned) by the council. Strong brand awareness. Consumers of mass-market products and entertainment.
Challenge for the church: Church attendance has often been out of tradition or religious duty. Now church competes with many alternative mass-market consumer activities.

Idyllic secluded
Choose environmentally attractive homes even if it means a long commute to work. Like nostalgia, watch less TV.
Challenge for the church: May be wary of long commuting to church. Might choose a local church even if there is little life.

Solutions for individuals

Build more relationships
Decide who you're going to invest your life in. Use the FRANK[28] categories below to identify who you could develop your relationships with further:
(Note: a developed relationship need not mean best friend. Depends on the context.)

Friends – existing, lapsed and potential. Often the easiest relationships to develop are with people you already know – especially people from the past who are on your Christmas card list but you don't see that often – go through your address book and give people a ring to catch up. Go for a drink or a meal. Organize a reunion, etc.

Relatives – how often do you see them?
Associates – how could you develop your relationships with colleagues to the point where it is natural for you to talk about spiritual matters with them?
Neighbours – living in your street, working at local shops, working out at local gym etc.
Kids – parents of your children's friends.

Add another person to your day
If you're already doing an activity that others would be interested in, why not invite them along? For example:
– A local cultural event / festival
– A day trip to the country
– A barbecue
– An evening at the cinema or theatre
– Watching a sports match live or on TV.

Go the extra mile in your communities
If the statistics are true, then the community in which you live will be full of people who are feeling isolated and in need of a friend. As Christians we can take the initiative and show sacrificial love, giving without expecting anything in return. Who are our 'neighbours'?
– At work
– In our network of acquaintances
– In our neighbourhoods
How can we meet their need of friendship?

Take up a sport or hobby
When I was a theological student I went to woodwork classes to meet local people. I got a great doll's house for my daughter out of it, but hardly any conversations. People went to the class, worked on their piece and then drove their cars home. Inviting them for a drink when the only words I'd said to them were 'Can I borrow your jigsaw?' didn't really work!
It's important to pick an activity that involves interaction with people:
– Playing team sports or a club sport in which you partner different people (i.e., not round-the-world solo yacht racing!)
– A hobby that involves meeting up with others to swap ideas
– An evening class in which you do more than just sit in a seminar room
(e.g., drama or creative writing, which both involve sharing work and getting to know each other).

Go to the pub

In our age of gated communities, people's homes are more castle-like and isolated than ever. As a result, places people go to meet each other play an increasingly important role. And, as Christians, we need to be there:
– In the local shops and coffee bars
– Having a drink or playing a game of darts at the local pub
– Taking the kids to the local park or playground.

Be a strategic consumer

We all have to eat food, get dry cleaning done and so on. By using particular shops and service providers we build relationships with them and, as we do that, those people will get to know we're Christians and opportunities will naturally arise for us to share the hope within us. It was a privilege for us to be there to offer support to our local chip shop owner when his wife was dying of cancer. We also had the opportunity to share the good news of Christ with the owner of one of the printing firms the church uses.

Get training and support[29]

Gain an understanding of:
– How to go into the world each day not just as someone who happens to be a Christian but as a gospel ambassador with an intentional missionary mindset
– How to build genuine incarnational relationships
– How to use church events as opportunities to bring friends.

Get praying

Ensure that prayer for people who are not yet Christians is always an item at every small group.
– Get into a prayer triplet to pray for each other's contacts.
– Meet as Christians at a firm to pray for colleagues.
– Meet as parents at a school to pray for the school.

A. 531 scheme
– Write down the names of 5 people you know who know little about Christianity and regularly pray for opportunities to share the hope that is in you.
– Write down the names of 3 people with whom you've shared that you're a Christian and regularly pray for an opportunity for them to hear the gospel explained (by you or at an event you take them to).
– Write down the name of one person who's heard the gospel but is not yet a Christian and regularly pray that he or she will make a step of faith.

B. 111 scheme
Ask every person in your church to pray for one person they know who doesn't yet know Christ for one minute at 1 p.m.
– imagine the power of Christians across the country doing that in unison! This can be extended to praying for more people if a different person is prayed for each day of the week.

Start a group at a local school

(Suggestions by Charlotte Baughen, age 14, who began a Christian club called Connection at her school)

It is usually helpful to have a child that goes to both the school and your church to help you find out the following:

1. What other similar groups there are at the school
2. When and where you could hold the group
3. Who to ask for permission to hold the group
4. What kind of format the child thinks will work best in the school.

You need to get permission to hold a Christian group from the appropriate person who has the correct authority.

You need to choose when the best time is to hold the club. It will most likely be at lunchtime or after school.

Plan the format for the group. Who do you want to come to the group – people who already go to church or people who might be interested in finding out more? Will you have talks or Bible studies? Who will run them? A Christian teacher may be prepared to run them, or your church children's worker may like to run the group.

Advertise in your school. This is a very important thing to do. You can use posters and notices in assembly and the registers. If you don't advertise well then people won't know about the group and won't come.

Lastly, make it a fun and warm environment for kids to be able to learn more and feel able to invite their friends to without it being embarrassing or sad.

Solutions for churches

1. Build visibility of church as a place of community
(knocking down the 'isolated' barrier)

A. Invest in people
Review what proportion of your financial resources, buildings, staff time and volunteer time is invested in people not in contact with Christ.

Are you investing in people, not buildings?

B. Door to door
There is still great benefit in face-to-face conversations with local people. In secure estates it may be very hard to cold call, but the more contacts you develop with people living in the estates, the more access you will have to other residents. Christians on the estates are your missionaries in those places.

Calling with a specific offer, such as the Jesus video for them to watch, can also be a helpful opening. Calling as an official representative of the church (maybe with identification) and perhaps asking if there is anything the church can pray about for them is another way of showing genuine care and concern for people.

C. Leafleting
Leaflets are not as effective a way of inviting people to services as personal invitations, but a regular distribution of attractively designed publicity builds awareness of the church's existence and the fact that the church is there to serve local people. It's a good idea to take care that the design shows that the church is about people – and not just another pizza leaflet!

Hand delivery is becoming increasingly difficult in secure estates. Mailshots may be more effective. It is usually best to hand address the envelopes if possible, but the name of the resident shouldn't be used unless they are personally known by the church. This removes any fear that they are being held on a database and ensures that it's not addressed to the wrong person.

D. Drop-in café

If the church is in a location where locals pass by frequently, opening a café may create opportunities to meet and serve them. This can be done as a once a week volunteer-run event, for example on a Saturday morning, rather than as a full-scale café – which has much bigger financial and staffing implications. For some churches with a more remote location, operating a shop or café in the local shopping area may be an attractive proposition.

E. Office base

Instead of church staff working from home, there are advantages to them working in a church office so the church building can be kept open and there is someone available through the week should someone pop in for a chat.

F. Use of building

Allowing local groups to use the church building enables people to become familiar with where the church is and to pick up leaflets and view information on notice boards.

G. Street band / drama

Rather than expecting local people to come to the church, a starting point can be for the church to go to them – with street theatre or music, for example.

H. Vox pops

Conducting video interviews on the street, which are then shown at church services, can create opportunities to meet people and invite them to come see themselves on the big screen. It also communicates to local people that the church is interested in what they think about current issues.

I. Profile in local media

Adverts – newspapers, magazines, posters, local radio, etc.
News articles – in local paper or radio.
Faith slot / thought for day – in local paper or radio.

J. Publicity for local services provided

Advertising leaflets / posters placed in schools, community centres, doctors' surgeries, libraries, etc. Operating a stall at local festivals. Listing in helpline services. Hosting local groups who then see posters, pick up leaflets.

K. Resources for current members to give out

Provide 'goodie bags' which 'hopper' church members can give as a welcome to people moving into their neighbourhoods. The box from the church could contain local maps and other information, details about the church, an invitation to a meal, a tape or CD (or voucher for the church resource centre), etc. Church members could present new neighbours with the goodie bag along with a meal or offer of help with unpacking, etc.

L. Regular social events

Activities such as a well-run toddler group or friendship hour for retired people will draw people during the week and are easy events for 'local' and 'hopper' church members to bring their friends and neighbours to.

M. Special social events

Special events for people with a particular interest or occupation or for those who have come from another country to work or study can work well because people with a common interest are more likely to socialize and it is easier to establish a theme for the evening. For example:
– A talk based on a specific common interest or occupation
– An event with food, music and other people from their home country.
Advertising events attractive to certain people is easier when there are specific publications they read or places they look for news.

N. Mailing list

Establish a 'friends of church' mailing list of people with an affinity to the church who are not ready to come on Sundays but may accept an invite to a social event as a first step.

O. One-off social events

People who live further away (contacts through friendship networks or neighbours of 'Commuters') are unlikely to come to regular social activities such as a drop-in café or weekly toddler group. But they may come to a one-off activity such as a meal or barn dance or festival event if invited by a friend or neighbour from the church.

P. Magazines

A good way of maintaining contact and informing people about the church is a regular magazine designed as a good read for people outside the church which gives a positive message about the church and seeks to remove any negative impressions people may have. It enables people to find out what the church is about and who's involved before they visit.
Magazines and/or leaflets can be sent quarterly: March (Easter), June (summer), September (new school year), December (Christmas).

Q. Welcoming strategy

– Information and welcome pack (could include a tape, DVD or CD with a welcome message, gospel outline, sample music).
– Welcome cards – in the seats or a tear-off section of the weekly bulletin.
– Welcome team that facilitates the welcoming by the whole congregation. Welcomers act as points of contact that new people can go to and also ensure that new people are introduced to others.
– Welcome desk with a team, information, refreshments, etc.
– Welcome slot where people are encouraged to greet their neighbour, and regular members know their job is to shake hands with a new person and then talk to them again as soon as the service is over, making sure they get a coffee and meet others.
– Welcome event such as a meal with a brief presentation about the church and what's on offer.

Solutions for churches

2. Develop expressions of church suitable to the context it aims to reach (knocking down the 'liquid' barrier)

A. Specific prayer

Meet regularly as a church to pray for the communities you are aiming to reach. Feed the prayer times with information so people can pray specifically for the context – for the issues and people known, for openings to meet people, for wisdom in being thoroughly contextual as well as distinctly Christian.

B. Missionary small groups

Encourage each small group to adopt an area or people network and pray for them. Gain an understanding of the issues they face and how the group could meet some of their needs. If appropriate, spend time as a group doing the things they do, going to the places they go. Meet as a group in a venue they meet in or nearby. Get to know them as a group and then organize a group event they would like to come to.

C. Website

Increasingly, people are using the internet to search for churches. Someone's first impression of your church may well be a virtual one. People also often use websites to check out churches they've spotted in their area. They may use the church notice board to learn the name of the church and then use the internet to investigate it in the comfort of their own home. A well-designed website will detail what the church offers, what style and approach the church adopts and will help people decide to come along to a service or activity.

D. Design

Using a consistent and carefully planned design on publicity you send out, notice boards you place at your entrance, leaflets you hand out and websites will give people a positive first impression. Whether it's planned or not, the design of publicity speaks volumes about your church – contemporary, classic, old-fashioned, arty, warm and friendly, down at heel, high or low on caring about quality, and so on. Any logo you might use also communicates what you're about – is it of a building rather than people, for example? Consider what your logo communicates to the outsider.

E. Develop fresh expressions of church appropriate to each group

If you have contact with people who would never feel at home at events or services you put on, however welcoming you are – people for whom the barrier isn't that they don't know any Christians, but rather that they don't know any Christians with whom they can identify – then a solution is to establish a fresh expression of church appropriate for them. There isn't any point contacting people if you're going to invite them to try out something inherently alien and therefore unwelcoming to them. Is your church at risk of being 'institutionally unwelcoming'?

Establishing a fresh expression of church may enable you to reach people previously unreached by your church. It's church built from within an unreached group's specific cultural context rather than your own. Fresh expressions of church need to do what they say on the tin: they need to still be about church – with the same theology of being a gathering of God's people under God's word with God's missionary commission – but freshly expressed for the communities they serve and grow out of.

The examples of 'fresh expressions' of church given on the next page are relational bridgeheads which aim to establish a church around a specific situation. These churches grow, therefore, as contact is made with people who are invited into a community in which they feel sufficiently safe and at home to start exploring faith. In effect, the planted church acts as a 'vortex' of solid biblical community – drawing people in from the liquid world it exists in. Examples of church communities that start with a homogeneous nuclei of people sharing a life stage context and then branch out:

– A group of parents with children under five who go to a toddler group at a church get together for a pram service and a church community develops
– A group of Christians runs a special event for residents of a sheltered housing development and they grow together into a church community
– A youth group develops a regular service to which they can bring their unbelieving friends.

Examples of church communities that start with homogeneous nuclei of people sharing an affinity context and then branch out:
– A church community develops for those interested in alternative styles of worship or particular styles of music and culture
– A church community develops out of a group meeting in which members help each other recover from addictions
– A church community develops out of a set of parents with children at the same school who see each other frequently
– A church community develops out of a cell group which effectively draws local people in.

Fresh expressions of church built around a homogenous nuclei of people sharing a common life stage or affinity have the challenge of long term sustainability. Over time the church of homogeneous seekers will become a church of maturing believers and they will naturally start inviting friends and family who may not share their starting point life stage or affinity. As it matures therefore a church's freshness of expression may broaden and become less about a particular homogeneity and more about a freshness of approach appealing to a wider community. At that stage you may find again that some groupings of people not yet Christians begin to feel disenfranchised from the church. One solution might be to start a new fresh expression of church or to establish evangelistic activities based round homogeneous life stages or affinities which all feed into a more heterogeneous church.

Fresh expressions of church described in the Mission-Shaped Church report:[30]
– Alternative worship communities
– Base Ecclesial Communities ('a church of the poor for the poor')
– Café church
– Cell church
– Churches arising out of community initiatives
– Multiple and midweek congregations
– Network-focused churches
– School-based and school-linked congregations and churches
– Seeker churches
– Traditional church plants
– Traditional forms of church inspiring new interest
– Youth congregations.

Additional suggestions of Fresh Expressions:[31]
– Fresh expressions focused on children or on under-fives and their families.

'[People ask] "aren't new expressions of church, for example, just an updated version of house churches, now known in Britain as 'New Churches'?"... The big difference, at least to emerging church in its mission mode, is that many New Churches continued to operate on a "you come to us" model. Members liked their new way of being church and used evangelism to encourage non-churchgoers to join them... Emerging church is not quite the same as church planting either, although planting is at the heart of it... Sometimes plants merely cloned existing church. A group of Christians might move onto a housing estate or into a school, start perhaps a more relaxed version of mainstream church and then issue the invitation, "Come and join us"... Emerging church with a mission heart is different. It does not start with a pre-determined mould and expect non-churchgoers to compress in. It begins with the people church is seeking to reach, and asks "What might be an appropriate expression of church for them?"'[32]

Solutions for churches

3. Build accessibility of church for all (knocking down the 'multi choice' barrier)

A. Offer a spiritual health check

To take an idea from a gym, develop a spiritual health diagnostic tool which people could either use with friends or could be on offer for a limited period at the church or a community centre or gym.[33]

B. Support new members in getting involved

People will feel more part of a church and less like an occasional consumer if they have a role within that group. Even if someone is not a Christian and not therefore able to take on a ministry role, there are plenty of volunteer opportunities. By joining a volunteer team a person makes some level of commitment to the church, takes a stake in the life of the church and gains the experience of community in a team which meets regularly for teaching and support.
– Introductory course covering what a Christian is, what the vision of the church is and how to get the most out of being a part of what goes on.
– Newcomers group: a 'holding' group that meets at the same time as the established home groups of the church with an open invitation for anyone new to attend. This group provides an opportunity for newcomers to receive immediate support whilst they are helped to find the most appropriate group and / or service opportunity for them to settle in more permanently.

– 'Volunteer fair': a series of stalls set up before and after services where people can get information on the different service opportunities at the church – how they might get involved and what it would entail. Such an event is often linked to a special teaching emphasis in the service.

C. Respond effectively to contacts about weddings, funerals and baptisms

These events can provide great opportunities to develop long-term relationships with local people. Decide a strategy, asking:
– How can the church reach out to those who are bereaved – before, during and after the funeral service? What sort of preparation courses and support can you offer to engaged and newly married couples? How can the church celebrate with, and serve, those with new babies?
– Should the church send cards on anniversaries?
– How can people find out what the church offers?

D. Offer a church 'taster' event

Rather than establish a fully fledged fresh expression of church for a particular grouping of people, it may be more effective to offer 'taster' events where they get an idea of what church is about, what the Christian message is about and what other Christians are like. These events might be a monthly 'seeker presentation' and maybe a different time from the main church services and in a different venue. These events allow a low commitment 'stepping stone' for people unused to church and can be much more specifically tailored to their preferences and needs.

E. Plant accessible church gatherings

On the previous page we looked at the option of developing a fresh expression of church within a particular cultural context in which your church already has a bridgehead of relationships. But there may be groups who will remain unreached – not because the culture of your church is a barrier, but because convenience is a barrier. In that case, planting a congregation in a location more easily accessible to 'multi choice' Christians and their friends may be an effective option.

There are many forms of church plant, but they all share the principle of making church more accessible.

This may mean meeting at a more convenient time:
– Midweek church in the evening or lunchtime
– After-school club followed by brief church 'service' when parents come to pick up their kids
– Saturday early evening church (pre-clubbing, but not Sunday night when people are getting ready for the working week)
– Various times on Sunday: 9.30am (rest of day free); 11am (lie in); 1pm (over lunch); 5pm (still have an evening); 7pm (back from weekend away); 9pm (more club feel).

Or meeting at a more accessible location:
– Near other Sunday leisure activities such as sports or shops
– Church meeting in a café or other secular / informal venue
– Where parking or public transport is easy (by a transport hub)

– Satellites and multi-location: same service content but presented in different styles (music, language, informality, etc.) in different settings.

Or a more accessible style:
– Church deliberately geared for people not familiar with Christianity
– Church for people for whom English is a second language.

Types of church plant:
– Reproduction: daughter church with distinct emphasis and independence
– Transplant: group going from big to small church
– Graft: similar-sized graft into existing group
– Ground-breaking: group moving to a new area to live and building a church by network evangelism
– Co-operative partnership: a group of churches get together to plant a new church
– Reboot: start again from scratch with a new leadership team or new vision or new strategy
– Satellites and multi-location
– Multi congregations: same location
– Midweek / lunchtime church
– Minster church: a 'cathedral type' flagship church that has a large staff team and draws people from a wide area and is able to put on a big range of programmes but also acts as a 'mother church' to local churches in its area by resourcing and being a central venue for those churches to come to for big celebration events, training, evangelism events, etc.[34]
– Outsourcing: people resources and skills lent by one church to another for a short- to medium-term

Expert witness

Interview with Mark Greene, London Institute for Contemporary Christianity

What do you think are the main barriers to unbelievers and believers building friendships with each other?

I agree with your suggested solution of consciously building more relationships but I think the idea of having a goal like 'make friends with people' is off-putting to Christians. A friend is someone who shares some of the deep things in my life, a friend is someone I have a fair amount in common with, a friend is someone who feeds my soul and whose soul I feed. It feels false to set out with a goal of making someone a friend. On the other hand, if you ask me to try to bless the people I meet, to celebrate who they are and help them along the way towards Christ, I can do that with integrity. They may become a Christian and we may become 'friends' but we may not. Besides, a non-Christian may not want me to be their best buddy, particularly if they're my boss. On the other hand, they may well be very open to being ministered to in quite a direct way.

Similarly, there are quite a lot of people I meet who would run to Kazakhstan if they thought I wanted to be their friend with a capital 'F'. But they would be happy to be invited along to a men's curry and beer evening with a few other blokes to discuss some relevant issue. Or go off to a football match with a few others. Or even come carol singing for charity.

One of the other barriers to effective evangelism is the false belief that I have to be the one to follow the relationship through. Maybe there's someone else who is meant to do that, someone who my non-Christian acquaintance would have a huge amount in common with – the music of Kurt Cobain, for example. Evangelism should be a body business and my role may simply be to introduce someone to another Christian.

What are your top tips for Christians who want to build relationships with unbelievers?

Pray. And look around – you probably already have lots of relationships with non-Christians – colleagues at work, parents at the school gate, neighbours and so on. Find a way to bless people that opens up conversations – bring in chocolate biscuits to work one day a week; pass on a press cutting about a topic you know they're interested in; think about the issues in their life – children, marriage, elderly parents – and perhaps offer a good book on the topic; start a reading group; invite people to a party – no tracts attached; invite them to do something you enjoy doing – watching the cup final, going to an aerobics class, crawling through cold, narrow, dark, dank, dripping tunnels a hundred feet underground. Or try out something you know they enjoy doing – one Christian I know jumped out of an aeroplane to help build a relationship with a colleague. But be honest, don't pretend to like things you don't.

What are your top tips for Christians who don't want to build relationships with unbelievers?

There could be lots of reasons why someone might feel that way – not least that they might think that God can't use them or that they're afraid of being caught out by a question. But if the reasons are more to do with social ease then maybe connect to someone who has relationships with unbelievers and offer to help them in some way – make the coffee, serve the drinks, do the shopping – and pray that God would bring a not-yet Christian into your life that you really like or whose life you can contribute to.

How do you get to know unbelievers?

I've got three children in three different schools so opportunities abound. Plus there are quite a lot of men who come along to our church who may not yet have a vibrant faith.

What difference does your faith make to your relationship with unbelievers?

My faith reminds me that they are hugely precious to God, all made in his image, all loved, all died for by Christ. My faith also reminds me that they are missing out on the wonder of a relationship with Christ right now, on the blessing he has for them now, as well as in eternity. So my faith motivates me to pray – not only for their salvation but for their well-being. My faith also makes me hugely grateful that Christ rescued me.

How can the local church help you in your work of befriending unbelievers?

Develop a programme of social events that non-Christians want to come to and where they can meet other Christians. And plan a menu of events that give not-yet Christians opportunities to explore Christianity more deeply.

Importantly, churches should not assume that adult Christians are confident to share their faith. Our research at LICC reveals that most don't. Which is, of course, why you've written this book.

Study Guide 2.

Study Scripture Jeremiah 24:7; Ezekiel 11:20; Zechariah 8:8;
2 Corinthians 6:16; Hebrews 8:10; Revelation 21:3
What does the phrase 'they will be my people' mean?
What does it tell us about God's ultimate purpose?

Study Scripture Ephesians 1:3–14
In what ways does Paul see the building of a people as God's ultimate purpose?

Apply: How does the mandate you have been given to build the people of God in your
setting shape your priorities as a church?

Study Scripture Luke 14:15–23
What principles does Jesus teach about why we should go and who we should go to?
How are the principles applied in Luke 10:1–20?

Study Scripture Acts 9:20–30; 14:1–18; 17:16–34
How is Paul's principle of being 'all things to all people' (1Cor. 9:22) shown in practice in
the different approaches he adopts?

Apply: What approaches will you need to adopt to be all things to all people in the
communities you are seeking to save?

Relationship building.

SCRIPTURE

SETTING 3

SOLUTION

Analyse your setting

1. Define your existing mix of members
- give % 'local', 'hopper' & 'commuter' and define key groups

2. Identify potential new 'local', 'hopper' & 'commuter' groups

3. Agree 'Focus Groups' God is calling your church to focus on building relationships with. Will you focus on groups you have a natural link with; groups God has already opened a door of opportunity with; groups you have the resources and ability to reach; cross-cultural groups no other church is reaching?

Focus group ....

Focus group ....

Focus group ....

Focus group ....

4. Gather data and build a profile on each 'Focus Group' (see solutions page 52 for details). Summary description of life stage and economic environment:

Focus group ....

Focus group ....

Focus group ....

Focus group ....

5. Analyse the barriers to building relationships:
Isolated, Liquid & Multi Choice Barriers
– What are the causes of isolation?
- How are relationships built?
- When and where do people spend their social time?

Focus group ....

Focus group ....

Focus group ....

Focus group ....

Relationship building solutions.

SCRIPTURE

SETTING

SOLUTION

3

Discuss and decide solutions
1. Values
How is Scripture driving your church's relationship building?
Encapsulate the scriptural mandate as a one sentence value:
'We build relationships with people because Scripture says...

2. Strategies
For each of your 'Focus Groups':
– How will you make your church known to them?
– How will you get to know them?

Focus group ....

Focus group ....

Focus group ....

Focus group ....

– Do you need to develop a fresh expression of church suitable to their context? How?

– Would planting a new church gathering reach more people and fit with their busy lives?

3. Goals
What goals will you set for the coming year?

What goals will you set for the next five years?

[1] John R.W. Stott, *Christian Counter Culture* (Leicester: Inter-Varsity Press, 2nd edn, 1978).

[2] David Bosch, *Transforming Mission* (Maryknoll, NY: Orbis Books, 1991).

[3] Chris Green, 'The Other Lord's Prayer' (London: Oakhill College and 9:38 Network).

[4] Leslie Newbigin, *The Gospel in a Pluralist Society* (London: SPCK, 1989).

[5] The Archbishops' Council, *Mission Shaped Church, Church Planting and Fresh Expressions of Church in a Changing Context* (London: Church House Publishing, 2004).

[6] All of the following statistics are from National Statistics Online (www.statistics.gov.uk). *Social Trends* 34 (2004 edn).

[7] 'Faith in Life' (London: Churches Information for Mission, 2001). A survey of 100,000 churchgoers throughout England on Sunday, 29th April 2001.

[8] Pete Ward, *Liquid Church* (Peabody, MA: Hendrickson Publishers; Carlisle: Paternoster, 2002).

[9] Ward, *Liquid Church*.

[10] Both quoted by Graham Cray, 'Allowing the Gospel to Grow the Church' (presentation at the Oasis Staff Conference, January 2004).

[11] Michael Nazir-Ali, *Shapes of the Church to Come* (Eastbourne: Kingsway, 2001).

[12] Cray, 'Allowing the Gospel'.

[13] Cray, 'Allowing the Gospel'.

[14] David Barrett is Professor for Missionmetrics at Regent University, Virginia Beach, and publisher of the *World Christian Encyclopedia*. He is quoted by Alan Hirsch, *A Journey to the Heart of Apostolic Genius*, Forge Mission Training Network 2004, downloaded from www.blahonline.net.

[15] Michael Frost and Alan Hirsch, *The Shaping of Things to Come: Innovation and Mission for the 21st-Century Church* (Peabody, MA: Hendrickson Publishers, 2003).

[16] Martin Robinson and Stuart Christine, *Planting Tomorrow's Churches Today: A Comprehensive Handbook* (Tunbridge Wells: Monarch, 1992).

[17] Rick Warren, *The Purpose Driven Church* (Grand Rapids: Zondervan, 1995).

[18] Cray, 'Allowing the Gospel'.

[19] Jon Rashbrook, pastor, Brookwood Community Church, Woking, Surrey.

[20] Jon Rashbrook.

[21] Nick Spencer, *Beyond Belief?* (London: LICC, 2003).

[22] Philip Richter and Leslie Francis, *Gone but not Forgotten: Church Leaving and Returning* (London: Darton, Longman & Todd, 1998).

[23] Simon Jones, *Why Bother With Church?* (Leicester: Inter-Varsity Press, 2001).

[24] Ward, *Liquid Church*.

[25] Michael Moynagh, *EmergingChurch.Intro* (Mill Hill, London: Monarch Books, 2004).

[26] For more information on researching neighbourhoods see Timothy J. Keller and J. Allen Thompson, *Church Planter Manual* (New York: Redeemer Church Planting Center, 2002).

[27] Categories and descriptions based on an article by Patrick Wintour, 'Voter Tribes: Marketing Pinpoints Audiences', *The Guardian* (28 December 2004).

[28] From Mark Ashton, seeker small group seminar (Wolverhampton, Willow Creek Conference, November 2003).

[29] See www.becauseapproach.com for updated resources for all solutions.

[30] Archbishops' Council, *Mission Shaped Church*.

[31] See www.freshexpressions.org.uk.

[32] Moynagh *EmergingChurch.Intro*.

[33] Based on an idea in Ward, *Liquid Church*.

[34] For more information see Nick Spencer, *Parochial Vision: The Future of the English Parish* (Milton Keynes: Authentic Media, 2004).

Matthew 5:16
Let your light shine before others,
so that they may see your good works
and give glory to your Father who is in heaven. (ESV)

Philippians 1:27
Whatever happens, conduct yourselves
in a manner worthy of the gospel of Christ.

1 Thessalonians 4:11-12
Make it your ambition to lead a quiet life,
to mind your own business
and to work with your hands, just as we told you,
so that your daily life may win the respect of outsiders
and so that you will not be dependent on anybody.

Respect building.

'Because loving churches attract attention.'

I don't normally learn many new things about evangelism from visits to motorway service stations, but I did the time I visited one with a friend who works for a car manufacturer. We were walking through the car park when he started pointing enthusiastically at something. 'Look over there! That's one of our most effective forms of advertising,' he said. I looked in the direction he was pointing, expecting to see some sort of all-singing, all-dancing billboard – but all I saw was a souped-up version of a very ordinary family car with fancy paintwork – a tea tray on the back and a skirt round the front. 'Is that it?' I asked. 'Yes,' he said, 'that car has been highly crafted with top-of-the-range parts. In fact, it's so expensive to adapt a sports edition like that from an ordinary car that we make a big loss on each one we sell. But it's worth every penny, because they are out-of-the-ordinary versions of something very ordinary. They act as moving billboards for our company.'

Christians should be the same – out of the ordinary, grace-filled versions of humanity. People who act as moving billboards for God. Being an advertisement for God 24 hours a day is a privilege, but also a responsibility – the Bible tells me to 'conduct myself in a manner worthy of the gospel of Christ' (Phil. 1:27). As the next verse says, people may well oppose us in many ways – but ultimately being like Christ brings glory to Christ by pointing people to Christ.

The staggering privilege Jesus gives his people is being adverts of his light to the world. God could have used many methods of advertising which we may think would have been more reliable, but he chose to attract attention to his light through his chosen people – you and me. Jesus describes his people as a city of light, shining bright in a dark world and lifted high for all to see (Matt. 5:14–16). Individuals shine the light of good deeds in daily life, and a gathered local church in a community acts as a 'stadium of God's light'. When people see 'your work produced by faith, your labour prompted by love, and your endurance inspired by hope in our Lord Jesus Christ' (1 Thess. 1:3), their attention will be drawn to the ultimate source and they will praise our Father in heaven – now that's what I call praise worth generating!

Because Jesus shows that God's character is compassion

In Luke's Gospel Jesus begins his ministry in his home town of Nazareth. He'd just spent 40 days in the desert thinking through the task before him and being tempted by the devil to take an easier option. So Luke 4 is Jesus' launch party speech – the moment when he publicly sets out his manifesto. What he says, therefore, is surprisingly and radically simple. There is no rousing speech about forming a revolutionary movement, no razzmatazz unveiling of plans to build a new 10,000-seat church complex on the outskirts of Jerusalem. Instead, Jesus' statement focuses entirely on people and their needs. Jesus reads the prophecy from Isaiah about the Messiah who will come and rescue God's people and says: 'That's me. I've come as the people's Messiah.'

From the beginning, therefore, Jesus shows that his heart is God's heart of compassion. Jesus sets out to do what God's people have always been told to do. As Moses said to the Israelites as they prepared to enter the promised land:
Deuteronomy 15:11 'I command you to be open-handed towards your brothers and towards the poor and needy in your land.'

Jesus obeys that command and publishes a manifesto all about meeting the needs of the poor and marginalized. In that Nazareth synagogue he proclaims the year of the Lord's favour to the poor, the prisoner, the blind and the oppressed – not the year of the dragon or the rat, but the year of the people. Jesus clearly states his intention to preach and proclaim an era in which people marginalized by economic, political, physical and spiritual oppression will know the transforming reality of the Lord's favour day by day.

Jesus instituted the era of compassion for the whole person, and he calls us to carry it on. Every Christian is to be a 'people person' – it's not an optional extra.

Luke 4
16 [Jesus] went to Nazareth, where he had been brought up, and on the Sabbath day he went into the synagogue, as was his custom. And he stood up to read. 17 The scroll of the prophet Isaiah was handed to him. Unrolling it, he found the place where it is written:
18 'The Spirit of the Lord is on me, because he has anointed me to preach good news to the poor. He has sent me to proclaim freedom for the prisoners and recovery of sight for the blind, to release the oppressed, 19 to proclaim the year of the Lord's favour.'
20 Then he rolled up the scroll, gave it back to the attendant and sat down. The eyes of everyone in the synagogue were fastened on him, 21 and he began by saying to them, 'Today this scripture is fulfilled in your hearing.'

Jesus is compassion incarnate. He became flesh and lived among us. He was tempted in every way. He didn't stay in smart hotels, fly into Jerusalem to give a lecture and then depart. He lived with people and in doing so showed light to them. So when Jesus tells his followers to be a bright shining city on a hill he's not asking them to do anything more or less than he did. Jesus is the Light of the World who shone in contrast to the surrounding culture and, when we live by his words, we will do the same.

VIP packages, which get you past the queues at nightclubs or into the premiere of a movie or even a walk on part on the stage, are increasingly popular. But it's a trend that isn't without critics. Some say that it devalues the perks for those with 'real' connections, while others argue that it debases celebrity status to a willingness to pay hard cash. Still others have said that the so-called VIP status is simply another way to get money out of people. Some VIP customers have complained that back-stage passes gain access to virtually nothing, others that the VIP pass may get you straight into a nightclub – but to sit down can cost £300 per table![1]

But Jesus didn't keep his compassion for VIPs only – nor should his church. Church is a place where everyone is a VIP, where VIP status is paid for by the Star of the Universe and everyone has a pass that gives him or her access to God himself!

Psalm 116
5The LORD is gracious and righteous; our God is full of compassion.

You are never more like Jesus than when you reach out and help someone.

We're very good at making excuses to opt out of things we don't want to do. Children learn the art from an early age. Adults may be more subtle, but we keep practising. As a result, we're very good at making excuses about why we can't be bothered to show much compassion. But, according to Jesus, 'people are my problem'.

Jesus came to serve people. At first everyone thinks this is great, but there is opposition as soon as the implications of his mission to people become clear. The crowd quickly turn when Jesus reminds them that God used Elijah and Elisha to meet the needs of people outside the nation of Israel. All of a sudden this mission to people doesn't seem so attractive – in fact, if 'people' includes everybody, it's positively repulsive to them.

Jesus never suffered from compassion fatigue – late into the night he healed people, all through the day he preached to all who would listen. He didn't put limits on when he was on compassion duty or who was on his compassion list.

Although there were millions of people on earth at the time, Jesus intentionally spoke the message of repentance and faith first to the Jews. He left the nations of the earth to his followers ('and did those feet...'? No!). But Jesus' compassion was not limited to Jews. When he saw a need, he didn't say 'sorry, but you're not on my job sheet for today'. His heart went out to all, including the occupying Romans (Matt. 8:5–13) and the Samaritan woman at the well (John 4:1–26).

When Jesus eats with despised tax collectors and touches unclean lepers he is showing his love without limits, and he is also teaching an important lesson about what it means to be God's people. Jesus demonstrates God's intention for his people to be a blessing to all people, not just to their own kind (Gen. 26:4), and to welcome other nations to come and receive God's grace. Jesus puts that into practice and points us to the reality of the heavenly banquet, with its radically multinational and multicultural guest list.

Because showing God's compassion builds respect for him

People can go to great lengths to stand out from the crowd, perfecting the art of being slightly different whilst remaining substantially the same. Clothes are a classic example. Most people want to wear the latest fashion that everyone else is wearing, but they shudder at the thought that they might turn up at an event wearing exactly the same thing as someone else. Our desire to be different is about subtle shades rather than substance.

Christians are people who are substantially different. Christian lifestyle never goes out of date because it's about a completely changed relationship with God that's exactly the same as it was in the swinging sixties of any century you care to mention.

1 Peter 2 describes the Christian church as being made up of individuals who have been completely transformed by God's mercy into the people belonging to God. Peter describes that change in terms of being called out of the darkness of separation from God into the light of relationship with him. Light and dark are the ultimate contrasts. That's why Peter urges his readers to remember the contrast. They need to recognize that they are strangers in a dark world – that because they are people of light, the darkness surrounding them is now alien to their very nature (v. 11). But, as well as a new reality, they also have a new responsibility to live a life of contrasting light. People will be pointed to God and glorify him, the Bible says, when they see the 'good deeds' of a transformed life (v. 12). A life that shows unconditional love leads people to look for the source – the cross of Christ.

The danger comes when the church of Christ stops being a contrasting light. Jesus clearly thought there was the possibility that we might crank down our contrast levels and hide the light of our life with God under a bowl so no one could see it (Matt. 5:15). The warning comes in the verses before, where Jesus says that if we lose our distinctive salty taste we're of no use to anyone.

1 Peter 2

9 But you are a chosen people, a royal priesthood, a holy nation, a people belonging to God, that you may declare the praises of him who called you out of darkness into his wonderful light.

11 Dear friends, I urge you, as aliens and strangers in the world, to abstain from sinful desires, which war against your soul. 12 Live such good lives among the pagans that, though they accuse you of doing wrong, they may see your good deeds and glorify God on the day he visits us.

Matthew 5

13 'You are the salt of the earth. But if the salt loses its saltiness, how can it be made salty again? It is no longer good for anything, except to be thrown out and trampled by men. 14 You are the light of the world. A city on a hill cannot be hidden. 15 Neither do people light a lamp and put it under a bowl. Instead they put it on its stand, and it gives light to everyone in the house. 16 In the same way, let your light shine before men, that they may see your good deeds and praise your Father in heaven.'

Deuteronomy 4

5 'See, I have taught you decrees and laws as the LORD my God commanded me, so that you may follow them in the land you are entering to take possession of it. 6 Observe them carefully, for this will show your wisdom and understanding to the nations.'

Joe is a frequent visitor to our church. He comes and uses a sink in the toilets as a shower (judging by the water he leaves on the walls), uses the church as a place to smoke (until we catch him) and always demands a drink. One day he came in and said to me, 'Give us a coffee and make sure it's got two sugars.' There followed a brief pause, as I didn't respond immediately, and then he said, 'Why are you looking at me with that xxx face?' I could have said, 'Because you didn't say please,' or 'Because I had a late night,' or 'Because I don't have the energy to clean up after you.' But the truth was I was looking at him like that because I didn't see him with the compassionate eyes Jesus does. So I simply said, 'Sorry, Joe' and put the kettle on.

People matter to God and ought to matter to us. But as we practise acts of compassion, it is important to remember:
▾ We are not just doing good deeds. We are seeing people with the compassionate eyes of God and following God's sacrificial example as we serve. He is our source of compassion and it's his grace we administer to his world.
▾ We want to meet spiritual as well as physical needs.

When Joe came into the church, asked for a coffee and then shouted at me, if I'd just said 'Sorry, Joe,' made him a coffee and nothing more, my love for him would still be only partial. True compassion means wanting him to be part of God's family of dearly loved and forgiven children – now on this earth as well as in the world to come.

The challenge throughout Scripture is to remain distinct so that people see the difference it makes to live life in relationship with God – and not praise us as being worthy of note but instead praise our Father in heaven (v. 16).

God's intention has always been that his people on earth would be an eternal blessing to others, inviting them to join Christ's eternal church. The people of God descended from Abraham were called to be holy as God is holy, and therefore to be so distinct from other nations that all would see God's blessings and seek him themselves (Gen. 22:17–18). As Balaam says of Israel in Numbers 23:21,23, 'the LORD their God is with them' and all will 'see what God has done!'

The challenge Moses gives to the people of Israel as they enter the promised land is to keep looking to God. They are not to forget to live by trust in him, thereby showing others that their God is wise and with them always (Deut. 4:5–8).

Jesus commands us likewise to be a blessing to others by going to the ends of the earth as witnesses to Christ (Acts 1:8). He prays that his church will be such a distinctive and loving people that others will come to know him (John 17). Churches have an awesome privilege – to be distinctive people of blessing to the four corners of their communities and beyond.

As churches we should be saying 'bless you' to our communities in action as well as words – and not just when someone sneezes!

Because churches are God's distribution network of grace

The book of Ruth is all about how God shows grace to a Gentile woman. He not only includes her among his people but also places her in the family tree that leads to King David and ultimately to Jesus himself. The book demonstrates God's compassion for people and presents a beautiful example of how God uses one of his people, Boaz, as a distributor of his grace on earth.

The widowed Ruth, from the despised nation of Moab, moved to Israel with her Jewish mother-in-law. In chapter 2, Ruth went to the harvest fields of her new home to glean grain that was left behind. She knew exactly who she was and what her rights were. Although in theory a foreigner such as herself had a legal right to glean, in practice she was dependent on finding a favourable landowner (v. 2).

But when Ruth met Boaz she met far more than grudging allowances. He referred to her as 'my daughter' (v. 8), encouraged her to stay and work with the others and offered her water. Later on, he invited her to join the harvesters' table and eat with them (v. 14). He fully included her and treated her generously. He even told his men to leave some stalks so that she could gather more than just gleanings (v. 16).

Ruth knew what she deserved and approached Boaz with suitable humility, face bowed to the ground. Ruth was surprised to receive so much more than she deserved. Her amazement is clear in every word she spoke to Boaz. 'I'm just a foreigner,' she said in verse 10, 'not even worthy of notice by you. Yes, as a non-Jew I can expect certain rights, but I never expected anything more – especially as a woman from the hated people of Moab.' His acts of kindness went way beyond the call of duty. As she said in verse 13, 'I do not have the standing of one of your servant girls.' But that's what compassion means – it means relating to people as valued individuals, not just problems, and responding to them out of love not just duty.

Ruth 2

2 And Ruth the Moabitess said to Naomi, 'Let me go to the fields and pick up the leftover grain behind anyone in whose eyes I find favour.' Naomi said to her, 'Go ahead, my daughter.' 3 So she went out and began to glean in the fields behind the harvesters. As it turned out, she found herself working in a field belonging to Boaz, who was from the clan of Elimelech. 4 Just then Boaz arrived from Bethlehem and greeted the harvesters, 'The LORD be with you!' 'The LORD bless you!' they called back. 5 Boaz asked the foreman of his harvesters, 'Whose young woman is that?' 6 The foreman replied, 'She is the Moabitess who came back from Moab with Naomi. 7 She said, "Please let me glean and gather among the sheaves behind the harvesters." She went into the field and has worked steadily from morning till now, except for a short rest in the shelter.' 8 So Boaz said to Ruth, 'My daughter, listen to me. Don't go and glean in another field and don't go away from here. Stay here with my servant girls. 9 Watch the field where the men are harvesting, and follow along after the girls. I have told the men not to touch you. And whenever you are thirsty, go and get a drink from the water jars the men have filled.' 10 At this, she bowed down with her face to the ground. She exclaimed, 'Why have I found such favour in your eyes that you notice me – a foreigner?'

When the epidemics hit the urban centres of the Roman Empire, the Christians showed their faith and compassion in practice by being willing to risk their own lives and stay in the cities to care for people. 'There was nothing new in the idea that the supernatural makes behavioural demands on humans – the gods have always wanted sacrifices and worship... What was new was the notion that more than self-interested exchange relations were possible between humans and the supernatural. The Christian teaching that God loves those who love him was alien to pagan beliefs... Equally alien to paganism was the notion that because God loves humanity, Christians cannot please God unless they love each other. Indeed, as God demonstrates his love through sacrifice, Christians must demonstrate their love through sacrifice on behalf of one another. Moreover, such responsibilities were extended beyond the bonds of family and tribe.'[3]

The revolutionary behaviour and love of the early Christians to all people at the time was noted by many pagan commentators. While the Emperor Julian loathed the Christians, he wrote in a letter in 362: 'The impious Galileans support not only their poor, but ours as well, everyone can see that our people lack aid from us.'[4]

The gracious acts and kind words Ruth received from Boaz left her with one key question: 'Why me?' 'Why have I found such favour?' she asks in verse 10. And Boaz's answer? Because of God's grace. As he says, 'May you be richly rewarded by the LORD, the God of Israel, under whose wings you have come to take refuge.' Boaz knew that the Lord has a vast wingspan of protection and delights to offer refuge to all who seek him. He also knew that the Lord's faithfulness to his people didn't stop – even when they were unfaithful towards him. The Israelites in the desert were outrageous in their complaints to God: 'We don't have enough food...we don't have any meat...we don't have enough variety on the manna menu...' and so their complaining went on. Yet, as the Bible points out (Neh. 9:19), God didn't abandon them in the desert – because he had compassion for them.

Boaz had experienced God's love many times, and his prayer for Ruth was that she would also experience God's love as she started her new life with God's people – people who were called to bless her and show her love that was not limited by family ties, restricted to a close circle of friends and servants, or defined according to racial groupings. God's people valued even a penniless woman from the enemy land of Moab.

The same should be true of God's people today. One thing is for certain – a church that practises God's love is bound to attract attention for all the right reasons.

Rodney Stark, who has made a detailed study of the early church, concludes that a major reason for its growth was the distinctive lifestyle of the Christians and their clearly higher moral standards. They loved each other and valued people outside the usual 'tribal' loyalties.

'What Christians did was take care of each other. Their apartments were as smoky as the pagan apartments, since neither had chimneys, and they were cold and wet and they stank. But Christians loved one another, and when they got sick they took care of each other. Someone brought you soup. You can do an enormous amount to relieve those miseries if you look after each other.'[2]

Because people often think Christians are weird or worse
(The 'weird Christians' barrier to respect building)

Nick Spencer's group interviews with a range of people from the 66% of the population who are neither convinced atheists nor definite believers in God found:[5]

1. The word 'religion' has negative connotations in today's society. People's word associations included: 'stuffy...discipline...brainwashing...grasping at straws'.

2. People tend to view Christians as a category as a little weird and out of touch. Word associations included: 'colourless...misfits...goody two shoes.' Or, as one person put it, 'If it's a lady [she'd be] sitting there with her cardie...and long tent like skirts...a terrible paisley-patterned one!'

3. Many of these people saw Christians as 'hypocrites' and 'intolerant':
'They like to think of themselves as kind of Christian but I think in my understanding of the word they're not.'
Christians are an easy target here because they declare that there is a moral code and they try to live by it, while others do not acknowledge any particular standards of behaviour against which they can be monitored.
'I just live my life as I believe I should live it, and make my decisions and hope they are good ones, and...have respect for other people.'
One of the reasons Christians are called intolerant is because the world often defines tolerance as accepting that there is no truth, that no one does anything wrong. But, in fact, Christian compassion is perhaps the finest expression of tolerance. Tolerance was the one principle the people surveyed could agree on:
'I think being Christian is being tolerant of everybody else.'

4. People surveyed also expressed mixed opinions about Christians they knew. Some gave positive examples of the love they'd been shown or the love between Christians that they'd observed. Yet people can view even expressions of Christian love with suspicion or cynicism.
'They want you to come and do their sessions...they are saying, "Do you have any questions about God?" "No, I've just come here to play with my child."'

'One of the hardest bits for me when I became a Christian was working out how to tell my non-Christian friends and colleagues. I don't think I was prepared for some of the disappointment. They just thought I was weird. I remember one time [at work] and I hadn't managed to tell anyone I was a Christian yet. But I did at that point and said I was going to church on Sunday and one of my friends started bleating at me like a sheep and then the other girl who was there started doing the same. "Bah you're just a sheep, you're just following, you don't know what you're doing." It was quite a shock for me to find my good friends suddenly turn and suddenly very anti something very dear to my heart.'[6]

A new breed of rock star: Quietly Christian

'It was easy to believe the devil had the best music when Britain's only Christian pop star churned out such songs as "Mistletoe and Wine". But unlike Sir Cliff, a new generation of Christian artists taking over the charts is blessed with youth, beauty and critical acclaim. Just don't ask them to talk about their faith... The NME editor, Conor McNicholas, believes there is a simple reason why rock stars don't talk about their faith: "The problem with religion is it's never cool. At the heart of all religions, there's a notion of control, and that's the opposite of rock'n'roll. It ends up being the least rock'n'roll thing you can think of. What people want from music is inspiration and escapism. Religion offers that in a very different way. Most people are looking to escape from that, it turns them off.'[7]

So what?

People will not be willing to look into the truth of the gospel of Christ until some of their false presuppositions about followers of Christ are removed.

To generate momentum you need three factors: direction, mass and energy.

For a church's influence on friends and neighbours to gain momentum requires the same three factors.

Direction

– knowing what it looks like to love with the compassion of Christ.

Mass

– a depth of relationships within the church and within our communities.

Energy

– it's hard work being different and, by definition, showing sacrificial love will be costly. Our natural tendency is to remain in our cliques, maybe just loving the more lovable people we meet. But if we're going to influence our area with the gospel we'll need the energy to break out of our comfort zones.

step 1. Preparation.		step 2. Relationship building.			step 3. Respect building.	
Strategy expertise	Strategy process	Isolated	Liquid	Multi choice	Weird	Insular
Preparation solutions		Relationship building solutions				

Because people's impression of church is 'not for me'
(The 'insular Christians' barrier to respect building)

When Sting sang the line 'I've lost my faith in the holy church' he wasn't alone. Confidence in church as an institution has radically altered in the past two decades:[8] In 1981, 5% of people surveyed had a net positive attitude to the church.
By 2000, 22% had a net negative attitude to the church.

Many people have little or no experience of church, and the ideas that church is 'a club for the faithful few' and 'I wouldn't be welcome because I'm not very religious' are common misconceptions.
Two-thirds of British adults surveyed believe that pubs have more to offer communities than the church. A third of adults visit their local once a week; only 7% are regular churchgoers.

Hostility to the church and to Christians is not a new phenomenon, nor is it unexpected. But such opposition does seem to be more overt now than it was in recent generations, and there is much less pressure to be seen as a churchgoer.[9]

1. The newspapers are full of articles that are openly critical of the church.

2. Young people are far more willing to identify themselves as belonging to no religion and attend church much less often than older generations:[11]
People who said in 1999:
– They belong to no religion or were not brought up in a religion

Age 18–24	27%
Age 65+	2%

– Attend one or more service a week

Age 18–24	5%
Age 65+	15%

A demonstration of the media's hostility to the church is given in this article entitled 'Oh, Lord. Not you again':
'Enough with the God, already... When I think of reasons I am proud to be British, number one is that just about nobody goes to church any more.
What a grown-up, intelligent, nation we will become, I think, when one day everybody takes responsibility for his or her actions. When simple morality about treating people with respect is not preached from a pulpit but resides in every family home, self-learnt and as instinctive as blinking... Idealistic, I know, but what can I say – I'm a believer.'[10]

One of the first things I did when I began at St James was to remove a painted sign on the church steps which read 'Do not sit or eat here by order of the churchwardens'. Instead, we cordoned off an area of the steps with plant pots and invited people to sit there. At lunchtime and in the evenings people from the church would sit with them and get to know them – the designer of this book cover was one of the people I met who has since become a dear friend.

But our policy was not universally accepted. One local couple told me it was 'disgusting...you came from the city and are just interested in turning the church into a money making business'. Over time, that couple have also become friends – they still don't agree about our use of the steps, but they do respect what we're about because they've seen, amongst other things, the love and care our youth team have poured into their son and other local kids. Over the years we have shared our lives and have wept together at funerals, celebrated together at their marriage renewal service and laughed together at community events.

'We have located ourselves in the building, the meeting and the programme and we have not effectively engaged the creation that holds our inheritance.'[14]

So what?

As churches we cannot take it for granted that we will be seen as a service to the community – by some we will be seen as the opposite. We need to earn the respect of outsiders by conducting ourselves in a manner worthy of the gospel.

There is a tendency to be reactive rather than proactive in talking about faith.

When 100,000 English churchgoers were asked which statement best described their readiness to talk to others about their faith, the top four responses were:[12]

Seek opportunities	12%
If it comes up	52%
Find it hard	20%
Life and action suffice	12%

In the film *Sister Act*,[13] Whoopi Goldberg witnesses a murder and is put into police protection with a new identity as a nun. The convent she hides in is linked to a local church where the priest admits, 'We're a small congregation this morning. Too many mornings. Something has gone terribly wrong. Where is faith? Where is celebration? Where is everyone?'
But things change when Goldberg starts to lead the choir. Afterwards the Mother Superior, played by Maggie Smith, makes her feelings known about the change of style.
The Mother Superior attempts to stop things there, but the priest intervenes by congratulating Goldberg and admitting he hadn't enjoyed mass that much in years. The changes attracted others off the street as well. As the priest says, 'That music, that heavenly music, Reverend Mother, it called to them.'

Because the impact of Christians is often missed
(The 'hypocritical Christians' barrier to respect building)

The UK government wants to encourage 'community champions' to act as the social cohesion glue that will bring communities together. Christians are often the 'social entrepreneurs' who are investing in, and actually living in, a community. The professional carers often live elsewhere and travel into a community. It's the people from the church who can be found in the shops and at the school gates and in the park at weekends.

Churches in the UK employ about 7,500 youth workers – that's three times the number employed by the government. Research also shows that Christians are three times more likely than non-Christians to involve themselves in the local community on issues that don't directly affect them. That's true for 27% of Christians[15] – which begs the question: What about the other 73%?

So what?
Christians are called to be radically different from the world – citizens of heaven who are recipients of mercy and who offer the spiritual worship of transformed lives. The Bible is clear that Christians should expect to be misunderstood and even persecuted.

But misunderstandings can be overcome. Paul tells the Thessalonians to make it their ambition to live lives that 'may win the respect of outsiders'. We clearly are not to expect that others will regard Christians favourably. Christians need to win respect by living in a way that deliberately seeks to break down barriers of misconception:
– By being transparent about our failure and need for grace
– By speaking of our true hope with gentleness and respect (1 Pet. 3:15)
– By showing the reality of a gospel life lived in step with the Spirit
– By demonstrating genuine interest, long term, in the lives of others.

'I realized we didn't need to be slicker or trendier to draw people in our community to Christ, but better and holier. We didn't need to invest time and money into more events but reinvest it into equipping our people to live genuinely good lives. We didn't need to be more religious; we needed to be more connected... I decided I would put much less time into pointing out the world's errors and much more time into proving God's love.'[16]

'People now know that Jesus, from whose face the light of the knowledge of the glory of God shines, is alive. To their surprise they see this Christ in these seemingly ordinary saints. It compels them to ask after and call forth the hope that God has placed within them... How different it is from that time when the gospel first "broke into" the city. This time is the time of the "restoration harvest". This is because the third phase of the divine strategy speaks of a victory that arises from within the city... Our challenge is to take hold of a paradigm and a strategy that will enable the saints to move beyond the multiplication of meetings and on into their life and work in the entirety of the created order.'[17]

The early church had: 'high morals, superior lifestyles, good works, sacrificial acts of love. Against raging currents of opposition in the ancient world, the message of the gospel nevertheless exploded because it was built over a bridge of living proof.'[19]

'We need to engage with our culture from a position of strength, not desperation. If we are desperate to please, we appease.'[20]

One accusation of hypocrisy we need to take care to avoid is the perception the only reason we care for people is to get a contact name and address so we can invite them to an evangelistic activity. In that case social concern isn't concern for the person as much as a means to a different end. Although that end is eternally vital, we can be accused of being underhand, if we are saying we are doing one thing when actually our aim is something different.

Tim Keller suggests a useful corrective when he says: 'The proper model is not to see mercy as the means to evangelism, or to see mercy and evangelism as independent ends, but to see both word and deed, evangelism and mercy, as means to the single end of the spread of the kingdom of God... Mercy and evangelism are like smoke and fire – where one is, the other must be near.'[18]

If we believe in God's unmerited favour and want to follow the example of Jesus we miss out step 2 of the Because Approach at our peril!

Churches are a visible witness to Christ when they are at the centre of their communities, offering hospitality and social concern to a range of people groups in three key ways:
1. Celebrating as biblical community. Christians know the amazing gift of unconditional love from God. The only weird thing about church, therefore, should be that it's full of the most joyful people on the planet – a family who delight in knowing God's love and showing it to others.
2. Champion of the wider community. Churches should not be holy huddles cut off from the world. They need to know and promote their vital role in the world – Christians are the only people able to infuse communities with Christ's salt and light and offer Christ's life-saving grace.
3. Care in the local community. Christians are to win the respect of outsiders by showing Christ's compassion in action.

step 1. Preparation.		step 2. Relationship building.			step 3. Respect building.		
Strategy expertise	Strategy process	Isolated	Liquid	Multi choice	Weird	Insular	Hypocritical
Preparation solutions		Relationship building solutions			Respect building solutions		

Solutions for individuals

1. Demonstrate that Christians are fun to be around (knocking down the 'weird Christians' barrier)

A. Small group socials
– Small group meals or other social activities to which every member invites friends who are not yet Christians.

B. Being real
– Be more honest and open about the realities of your hopes, dreams, joys and concerns with friends who are not yet Christians. Show them that your faith is living and impacts daily life.

C. Get training
– Prepare your testimony ('the best spontaneity is rehearsed') and get training in how to use opportunities to witness.

2. Get involved in the local community (knocking down the 'insular Christians' barrier)

Research shows that when people become Christians, the centre of gravity in life-sharing friendships starts to move towards Christian friends. That movement can sometime get to the point where virtually all of a Christian's close friendships are with other church people. If we mix exclusively with Christians, then some things are certain:
– Our capacity for personal evangelism will be severely limited
– Our unbelieving colleagues at work, neighbours in our street and others we meet through them will have every right to think we're a bit weird and insular.
Ideas to resist the pull to insularity include:

A. 50:50 rule
– Consciously invite at least as many unbelievers as Christians to a social event. Ensure that the Christians don't just talk to other Christians.

B. Local groups
Be strategic about serving in the community – as a local school governor, on groups planning local festivals, advising on community services and projects and so on.

C. Prayer
Pray as you walk round your local area. Pray for the peace and prosperity of the community (Jer. 29:7) and for community leaders. Observe the people and needs of the community and ask for opportunities to serve them with Christ's love. If appropriate, offer to pray for people you meet – ask if there is anything they'd like you to pray for or have the church pray for.

3. Demonstrate the investment of Christians in the social capital of their communities
(knocking down the 'hypocritical Christians' barrier)

A. Get serving
In the business of daily life it's easy to miss some easy opportunities to show practical love to neighbours and friends. Ideas include:
– A welcome meal for people moving in locally (spot 'sold' signs and find out when people are moving / watch for a lorry)
– Offer free babysitting
– Offer to do some shopping
– Provide meals for new parents to help in the early days
– Invite the whole street or block to a meal, party, kids' sports competition or family sports day.

B. Make yourself known
It is to ensure that what people see is the genuine motivation of love for our Lord and his people that underpins everything we do. How can you therefore make known the hope that is in you? What are you known for? If a person you're in contact with had a leak he'd call a plumber. If she experienced a crime she'd call 999. What is the if they'd call on you for?

Solutions for churches

1. Demonstrate that Christians are fun to be around and relate to each other as family
(knocking down the 'weird Christians' barrier)

A. Social events open to all
Instead of planning every outreach event to specifically explain the gospel to unbelievers, a great starting point is to simply invite unbelievers to events where they can experience the distinctive reality of the gospel lived out in a church family. Invite church members to come and enjoy all the fun of the church family event – and encourage them to bring friends and neighbours so they can see that Christians are more fun, more loving and less weird than they might have imagined.

B. Fun days
– Church days out to the seaside / theme park
– Festivals in local parks or other open community spaces with barbecue, family games, bouncy castle and so on.

C. Midweek
Transform church meetings into church family gatherings where life sharing is enjoyed over food – in the early church, devotion to the fellowship included eating together with glad and sincere hearts (Acts 2:42,46).
Handy hint: As any company will tell you, meetings that begin with people eating together are far more relational than meetings that just get through the business so people can leave again.

step 1. Preparation.   step 2. Relationship building.   step 3. Respect building.

| Strategy expertise | Strategy process | Isolated | Liquid | Multi choice | Weird | Insular | Hypocritical |

| Preparation solutions | Relationship building solutions | Respect building solutions |

D. Sundays

Make services and other times church meets 'events' rather than people just coming to 'a service' and then dashing off:

– Breakfast before church

Handy hint: New people often arrive early for church, and if they go straight in they may well be greeted by an empty room because the regulars come later, or with a noisy room because people are rushing around testing mikes and practising songs. Breakfast in another area of the building is a friendlier and more disarming first impression of the church.

– Coffee after church

Handy hint: Many new people will leave right after the service if you expect them to go in search of coffee and then hold it in a large hall full of people they don't know. One idea is to have coffee on trays which are passed down the rows of seats as the service ends. If people are given a decent cup of coffee in a proper café-style heat-retaining paper cup they will at least stay long enough to drink their hot brew and therefore long enough for a member of the church in a nearby seat to have introduced themselves.

– Sunday lunch, supper, etc. on a regular basis which the whole church is encouraged to make a red-letter day

– Special talks on a current issue or a social event after the service at which people can meet others and discuss issues.

Solutions for churches

2. Get involved in the local communities (knocking down the 'insular Christians' barrier)

A. Culture

– Local history evenings, wine tasting, concerts, etc.

B. Sport

– Put on a football or other sports tournament

Handy hint: it is often more strategic to join secular teams or form a church team in which at least half the team are non-church members.

– Screen big matches

Case study: One of the first activities we did to show hospitality to our community was to screen the World Cup in 1998. We simply put a sign outside and, by the time England played Argentina, we had such demand that people had to come to the church office in person to pick up a maximum of two free tickets, so we ended up with hundreds of people coming into our building and getting the opportunity to chat with them. At the match, I simply said this was a way that we as a church could play host to the community – and if anyone ever wanted a vicar or a chat, 'I'm your man!' That got a round of applause and built a positive impression towards the church.

C. Facilities

There are great benefits to people coming into the church building for other events such as:
– Rentals for parties, keep-fit classes, ballet, etc.
– Hosting meetings of community groups, AA, etc.
– Providing space for uniformed groups, etc.
People coming to these events will gain a greater familiarity with the building, and they will see the church as playing a valuable role in local community life.

While using your facilities they'll gather impressions:
– The quality of the facilities removes the barrier that churches are tatty, old-fashioned and uncared for
– The warmth of the welcome by church staff, volunteers and other groups they meet in the building reduces the barrier that Christians are unfriendly or sanctimonious
– Attractive publicity for church events breaks down misconceptions by offering a picture of lively community.
(Of course, the caveat to the above is that tatty facilities or unhelpful church staff or members or out-of-date signs, such as Christmas posters still up in January, give a very different impression.)

Solutions for churches

3. Demonstrate the investment of Christians in the social capital of their communities (knocking down the 'hypocritical Christians' barrier)

Using the resources of a church to meet the needs of the community not met by other agencies 'establishes bridgeheads of communication with people beyond the reach of regular church activities'.[21]
The objective is to meet people where they are with what they need.

A. Social concern

Including: community work parties (decorating, home improvements and furnishing, improving estates, giving Christmas hampers, etc.); disability support; bereavement counselling; recovery from addictions (alcohol, etc.); recovery from divorce, etc.; visiting in prisons; projects for the homeless.

B. Freebies

Giving free gifts demonstrates grace and breaks down the preconceived barrier that churches are after your money.
Examples include giving coffee and snacks to commuters, car washing by the youth club, roasted chestnuts at a Christmas fair, a gift wrapping service at local shops.

Case study from the Hillsborough churches network: On three Saturdays before Christmas, Christians offer a free wrapping service to shoppers. They get the paper and ribbon, etc. donated by the shops. There is a Christmas prayer tree on which shoppers can write a prayer – these are then distributed amongst the churches. As they wrap, the volunteers talk to the shoppers and give them a card advertising Christmas events.[22]

Step 1. Preparation.		Step 2. Relationship building.			Step 3. Respect building.		
Strategy expertise	Strategy process	Isolated	Liquid	Multi choice	Weird	Insular	Hypocritical
Preparation solutions		Relationship building solutions			Respect building solutions		

C. Food

A café is a lot of work but can provide opportunities to listen to those in need and to chat with those who are lonely. Cafés can thus be seen as a compassion ministry rather than a money-making scheme.

D. Family life

Toddler groups, when they're led with the vision of a compassion ministry, can be more than just a way of meeting people. When the leaders and helpers are meeting to pray for the people attending and for opportunities to demonstrate sacrificial love to the participants, the activity becomes a key part of an overall evangelism process. It is a ministry that gives people a first taste of what Christ's love and community look like in practice. Examples of clubs and other family life activities include:

Toddler groups; after-school clubs; youth clubs; adoption support; dads clubs to see children; crisis pregnancy support; holiday kids clubs, etc.

E. Senior citizens

Activities could include: a regular group for elderly members to come and enjoy fellowship and perhaps a meal; a special week of events for the elderly, perhaps run in school holiday time so there are more volunteers available – in effect, a holiday club for the elderly linked to a special service at the end of the week.

F. Awards ceremonies

An annual dinner that celebrates and awards prizes to local people who have made particular contributions to the community gives profile to the church and its activities and networks with other service providers.[23]

Expert witness

Interview with Paul Perkin, Vicar of St Mark's Battersea Rise, London

What do you think are the main barriers to people respecting Christians and the church today?
The irrelevance and outdated nature of Christianity is a commonly held perception and the other one fed by the media is the hypocrisy, judgementalism and exclusiveness of Christians. Another big one is the common understanding that the real world is about facts and faith is about subjectivity and private opinion which cannot command public respect.

Why should a church and individuals seek to show the love of Christ in practical ways?
Mercy ministry needs to be kept distinct from evangelism. The framework I use to communicate with the congregation is that mercy ministries pave the way for the gospel and also follow as a consequence of the gospel. As a Christian is being sanctified, their awareness of others is awakened.

Mercy ministries demonstrate that Christians are not detached from the real world and break down the barrier that Christians are exclusive. The accusation of hypocrisy is also removed if love is seen in action.

How do you do that at St Marks?

In recent years we have tried to gauge much more accurately what the felt needs of people are – or at least what people think their needs are.

For example, our reconciliation work came out of identifying the number of conflicts going on in our area.

Alongside that, we're doing much more evaluation. We're willing to say this isn't achieving anything and move on – either because we can't meet the need or because the method we're using isn't scratching where they itch.

There's so much desire to do good, the danger is a knee-jerk reaction rather than careful assessment.

One new area is mediation in the community:

Peer group mediation – gangs or bullies at school

Neighbour mediation – dispute between next-door neighbours

Us and them mediation – the 'us' is people on an estate and the 'them' is anyone in authority who is thus perceived as a threat, be that police, school staff, housing department, etc.

We find the work by referral from an agency such as the noise control people or word of mouth and get a little from advertising.

We don't do marriage mediation because we've assessed that's best left to specialist counsellors and family lawyers.

Another productive area is debt counselling – how to manage money you've got and how to get out of debt.

Each ministry has an evangelistic goal – leaders are trained to lead on to evangelistic discussion. For example, mediation leads to consideration of reconciliation with God. Debt counselling provokes thought about other debts in my life, especially the debt of sin. Rather than mercy ministries being disconnected from the rest of church and just 'a good thing', we're looking to link them into a whole church concern for the whole person. A way into a spiritual need may be through a social need.

What difference has it made to your church?

It's provided a much bigger range of opportunities for service for people and broadened opportunities from internal church jobs to service in the community. It's also brought a greater breadth of people and concern into the church. Tonight we're baptizing a couple reached through these ministries and they bring their story to share, their background and eventually their friends – and the whole church benefits from that.

Study Guide 3.

SCRIPTURE
SETTING
SOLUTION
3

Study Scripture Psalm 146; Zechariah 10
What does God's compassion for people look like?

Study Scripture Isaiah 1; Zechariah 7
What should our compassion for people look like?
How do the Israelites lack compassion for people?
Why is it that they don't have God's heart of compassion?

Apply: What is our only source of true compassion for people?

Study Scripture 1 Thessalonians 2
Why did Paul share not only the gospel but also his life?
How did he share his life?

Apply: Ask yourself: 'Am I sharing the gospel and my life fully with the people I know?
Where are the gaps?'
Is your church sharing the gospel and your lives fully in the communities you serve?
Where are the gaps?

Respect building.

SCRIPTURE

SETTING **3**

SOLUTION

Analyse your setting
Analyse the barriers to building respect within each
'Focus Group':

Weird Christians barrier
– What presuppositions and misconceptions about
Christians need to be broken down?

Focus group ....

Focus group ....

Focus group ....

Focus group ....

Insular Christians barrier
– What presuppositions and misconceptions about the role of a church in a community
need to be broken down?

Focus group ....

Focus group ....

Focus group ....

Focus group ....

Hypocritical Christians barrier
– To what extent are Christians seen as making a positive and effective contribution in the
community?

Focus group ....

Focus group ....

Focus group ....

Focus group ....

– What issues identified in the analysis of economic environment (in Study Guide 2) could
the church address with practical actions?

Focus group ....

Focus group ....

Focus group ....

Focus group ....

Respect building solutions.

Discuss and decide solutions
1. Values
How is Scripture driving your church's respect building activities? 'We are showing compassion in our communities because Scripture says...'

2. Strategies
For each of your 'Focus Groups':
– How will you demonstrate to people that Christians aren't weird but are fun people to be around?

Focus group ....

Focus group ....

Focus group ....

Focus group ....

– How will your church resist the pull to insularity and get involved in your community?

Focus group ....

Focus group ....

Focus group ....

Focus group ....

– How will you demonstrate your investment in the social capital of your community?

Focus group ....

Focus group ....

Focus group ....

Focus group ....

3. Goals
What goals will you set for the coming year?

What goals will you set for the next five years?

[1] *Wall Street Journal* (14 May 2004).

[2] Interview by Michael Aquilina with Rodney Stark at www.touchstonemag.com.

[3] Rodney Stark, *The Rise of Christianity: How the Obscure, Marginal Jesus Movement Became the Dominant Religious Force in the Western World in a Few Centuries* (San Francisco: HarperCollins, 1997).

[4] Stark, *Rise of Christianity*.

[5] Spencer, *Beyond Belief?*

[6] Interview with Pauline Koelling, *Christianity Explored* videos, 'Exploring Christian Life: Programme 1, The Church' (London: All Souls Church, 2003).

[7] Owen Gibson and Patrick Barkham, 'A New Breed of Rock Star: Quietly Christian', *The Guardian* (29 January 2005).

[8] ORB, in *Quadrant* (September 2003), Christian Research.

[9] *The Week* (London: Dennis Publishing Ltd., 13 November 2004).

[10] Martin Samuel, 'The Thunderer', *The Times* (9 November 2004).

[11] Social Trends No. 31 (2001 edn) HMSO.

[12] 'Faith in Life'.

[13] *Sister Act* (Touchstone Pictures, 1992; video distribution: Buena Vista Home Entertainment).

[14] James Thwaites, *The Church beyond the Congregation* (Carlisle: Paternoster, rev. edn, 2000).

[15] Quoted by Steve Chalke at Word Alive, 2004.

[16] Robert Lewis, *The Church of Irresistible Influence* (Grand Rapids: Zondervan, 2001).

[17] Thwaites, *The Church*.

[18] Timothy J. Keller, *Ministries of Mercy: The Call of the Jericho Road* (Phillipsburg: P&R Publishing Company, 2nd edn, 1997).

[19] Lewis, *The Church*.

[20] Talk by Mark Sturge at The Stepney Area Clergy Conference, Merville, 2005.

[21] Monica Hill, Healthy Church.mag.uk (5 October 2004).

[22] CPAS, *Church Leadership* (www.cpas.org.uk).

[23] Quoted by Rick Warren at The Purpose Driven Church Conference, Saddleback Church, 2004.

John 1:9-10
The true light, which enlightens everyone,
was coming into the world. He was in the
world, and the world was made through him,
yet the world did not know him. (ESV)

step **4.**

Relevance
building.

'Because we mind the gap.'

One of the most terrifying scenes in London's Leicester Square at a weekend has to be the crowds of people that gather in costume for Sing-Along-A-Sound-of-Music. I enjoy *The Sound of Music* as much as the next person, but early on there's a song that always makes me want to weep in despair and shout 'No!' at the screen. When Maria leaves the nunnery to be a governess, she bursts into song on the bus with the words, 'I have confidence in sunshine, I have confidence in rain... I have confidence in confidence alone... I have confidence in me!' What rot! None of the things she mentions can be trusted with any degree of confidence. It's all very well singing about sunshine, but my life isn't always full of it and I don't necessarily have confidence it will be anytime soon. And it's no good Maria singing 'I have confidence in me' when the whole point of the song is that she lacks confidence in herself!

The tragedy is that the place where she should find confidence has let her down well and truly. Spending time contemplating God's word in the nunnery should have left her with a God-sized confidence. That's what Christian faith is all about. A Christian is someone who puts his or her confidence in Jesus, who can be fully trusted in all things. As a Christian I can sing another version of Maria's song: 'I have confidence in the Son of Man, I have confidence he reigns!' (1 Thess. 1:4-5)

One of the reasons I love chatting about Christian faith with people who are a long way from God is because it's so exciting to see the light switch on as they begin to see the eternal realities of God's amazing grace. Each of us can be involved in this exciting work – being a bridge builder connecting people on earth to heaven.

Christ calls out to his church today, in the words of the London Underground announcer, to 'mind the gap'. Mind the vast gulf of misunderstanding and lack of spiritual insight which is separating so many people from Christ. And Christ also calls us to help bridge the gap by connecting people living in a messy and broken world to the God who is fully loving, completely pure and never breaks his promises.

Because people in darkness need connecting to the Light

Isaiah 9 describes the problem: people are in darkness, experiencing the gloom of distress (v. 1), the 'death-like shadow' of troubles[2] (v. 2) and the burden of oppression (v. 4). There is a clear need and a clear solution: the mighty God will come as a great light (v. 2). His everlasting rule of justice and righteousness (v. 7) will be like the joy of harvest time after a long hard winter (v. 3). The light of Jesus won't just give a bit of light to some people for a little while – he will shatter the power of darkness (v. 4) and cast the tools of darkness into the fire (v. 5). The light will totally replace the darkness forever (v. 7). John says the same thing about the light in the first chapter of his Gospel. Jesus is the light who shines in the darkness (John 1:5) both as creator of light (v. 3) and saviour who restores the light of life in relationship with God (v. 12).

Being in the dark is never an option you'd choose on a permanent basis – unless you're a bat. John says the light is Jesus, who made all things. From the beginning his light of life has been shining. But the tragedy is that many people remain in the dark. Why? John mentions several reasons:

1. They don't understand the nature of the light.
What does light do? It allows us to see. Coming out of darkness into light is like arriving at a place in the dark and opening the curtains in the morning to see a wonderful view of the sea or mountains.
What does Jesus offer to do? He restores our sight on life (v. 4) – through Jesus we can see the reality that we were created in the image of a loving, purposeful God. He enables us to see that life is not a random stumbling in the dark. The problem is that if you've never known light you don't realize you're in the dark. Unless you've been introduced to the reality of light, it will be an irrelevance to you.

John 1
1 In the beginning was the Word, and the Word was with God, and the Word was God. 2 He was with God in the beginning.
3 Through him all things were made; without him nothing was made that has been made. 4 In him was life, and that life was the light of men. 5 The light shines in the darkness, but the darkness has not understood it.
6 There came a man who was sent from God; his name was John. 7 He came as a witness to testify concerning that light, so that through him all men might believe. 8 He himself was not the light; he came only as a witness to the light. 9 The true light that gives light to every man was coming into the world.
10 He was in the world, and though the world was made through him, the world did not recognise him. 11 He came to that which was his own, but his own did not receive him. 12 Yet to all who received him, to those who believed in his name, he gave the right to become children of God – 13 children born not of natural descent, nor of human decision or a husband's will, but born of God.

Before we can show people how they can bridge the gap between themselves and God we need to show them that there is a gap, and that it's serious. It's no use explaining God's solution until people accept the problem.

It's the point made in the film *The Matrix*.[4] Before Neo can be released from being a battery pack for the machines, he needs to understand the reality of what he is. Morphius offers to save him from the machines by giving him a coloured pill, but first Neo needs convincing – he needs saving. Morphius says:
'Let me tell you why you are here. It's because you know something. What you know you can't explain but you feel it. You've felt it your entire life. There is something wrong with the world. You don't know what it is but it's there, like a splinter in your mind driving you mad.'
The heartbreaking reality is just how true that is of us. We were created to live in relationship with Jesus, the light of the world, but many people instead consider the darkness of separation from God as normality. Being in the darkness can become so 'normal' that people get accustomed to the dark and forget about the glories of light all together. Our awareness of God is reduced to brief splinters of light – small reminders of a deeply buried longing. This glimpse of unconditional love seems so familiar and right, but at the same time we fear it because it's largely unknown.

2. They don't recognize the source of light.
Everybody puts their trust in something – the depressing reality is just how often people trust in imitations of the true light that ultimately offer no light at all. If sparkling diamonds are a girl's best friend, the Great Light of the world won't be. As long as we worship idols, we won't recognize the Creator and source of light in the world (v. 10). People are in darkness because they don't recognize Jesus as the light.

3. They don't receive the gift of light.
People are in darkness because they think they're OK without a relationship with God – he's just for religious people in need of a spiritual crutch. Darkness is the absence of light. The darkness Jesus removes is the absence of a relationship with him. The gift of light is the gift of restored relationship with God as our Father (v. 12). It's a gift we receive by believing in Jesus, and it's free. It's neither deserved nor a birthright (v. 13).

4. They don't want to face the light.
Light puts darkness in its proper perspective. In God there is no darkness at all (1 John 1:5), and in his light the dark evils of our lives are laid bare (John 3:19–20). Light and dark do not mix. People are in darkness because they hate the implications of light – 'don't you dare judge me'. As Paul says of the Jewish leaders in Rome when he quotes Isaiah (Acts 28:27):
'For this people's heart has become calloused; they hardly hear with their ears, and they have closed their eyes.'

In the film *Moulin Rouge*[3] Nicole Kidman sings, 'Diamonds are a girl's best friend'. But this material girl is really in darkness, and when the crowds are gone and she's alone she sings: 'I follow the night, can't stand the light. When will I begin, to live again?'
But the only way out of the darkness is to turn to the light.

Church is a lighthouse – a gathering of many individual lights into a shining city on a hill which points out the dark of the world, connecting people to the reality of the Light of the world.

Strategy expertise	Strategy process	Isolated	Liquid	Multi choice	Weird	Insular	Hypocritical

| Preparation solutions | | Relationship building solutions | | Respect building solutions | | |

Because there is a gap between our futility and God's eternity

In 1969 Samuel Beckett wrote the play *'Breath'*, which is just 35 seconds long. It begins with the quiet cry of a newborn baby. Then, as a pile of rubbish on the stage is gradually lit, there is the sound of an inhaled and exhaled breath. The play ends with the dimming of the light and an identical newborn baby's cry. For Beckett, life seems to be nothing more than a meaningless breath and a pile of rubbish.[5]

The quest for meaning is an ancient preoccupation. The book of Ecclesiastes plays the 'what if' game – what if there were no God? It uses the term 'life under the sun' to imagine the world from the viewpoint of an agnostic who believes in the words of John Lennon's 'Imagine' – that there's no God, and above us only sky. The book explores a bleak proposition through analysis and from bitter experience. By connecting to that supposed bright warm dream of human self-sufficiency, Ecclesiastes shows its reality as a cold dark nightmare. It pushes the logic of a God-free world to its ultimate pointless conclusion. Verse 2 of chapter 1 says it all.

Ecclesiastes concludes that, without God, we are:
– Trapped in the endless circle of life (1:5–7)
– Tricked by the illusion of the new thing (1:8–10)
– Forgotten by the march of history (1:11)
– Crushed by the inadequacy of wisdom (1:12–18)
– Not satisfied by money, sex or power (2:1–11)
– Defeated by the certainty of death (2:12–16)
– Stressed by the pointlessness of work (2:17–23)
– Abused by injustice and evil (3:16; 9:1 – 10:6)
– Oppressed, without comfort and alone (4:1–8).

But the book doesn't leave us there. It connects with an atheist worldview in order to show its inadequacy, to show the darkness of life under the sun when the Son of God is rejected and his light ignored. But into its dark conclusions comes the odd shaft of light – it seems that the author couldn't help stepping out of the 'what if' game for a moment to say, 'but of course that's not reality

Ecclesiastes 1
8 All things are wearisome, more than one can say. The eye never has enough of seeing, nor the ear its fill of hearing. 9 What has been will be again, what has been done will be done again; there is nothing new under the sun.
14 I have seen all the things that are done under the sun; all of them are meaningless, a chasing after the wind.

Ecclesiastes 2
22 What does a man get for all the toil and anxious striving with which he labours under the sun? 23 All his days his work is pain and grief; even at night his mind does not rest. This too is meaningless.
24 A man can do nothing better than to eat and drink and find satisfaction in his work. This too, I see, is from the hand of God, 25 for without him, who can eat or find enjoyment?

Ecclesiastes 3
10 I have seen the burden God has laid on men. 11 He has made everything beautiful in its time. He has also set eternity in the hearts of men; yet they cannot fathom what God has done from beginning to end.
14 I know that everything God does will endure for ever; nothing can be added to it and nothing taken from it. God does it so that men will revere him.

Ecclesiastes 12
13 Now all has been heard; here is the conclusion of the matter: Fear God and keep his commandments, for this is the whole duty of man.

In the film *About Schmidt* Jack Nicholson plays a recently widowed and retired insurance salesman who starts to wake up to the pointlessness of the life he's led. At the end of the film he writes a letter in his mind to a child he sponsors in Africa: 'I am weak and I am a failure. There's just no getting around it. Relatively soon I will die, maybe in twenty years, maybe tomorrow. It doesn't matter. Once I am dead and everyone who knew me dies too it will be as if I never even existed. What difference has my life made to anyone? None that I can think of. None at all. Hope things are fine with you. Yours truly, Warren Schmidt.'[6] After I heard that I wanted to stop people as they left and say 'That's not how it has to be – you can know the significance of a God who loves you so much that he gave his only Son so that you could know eternal life in relationship with him rather than perish as a pointless failure without him. That's what gets me up in the morning!'

There is an American reality TV show called *Extreme Makeover*. In the episode I saw, one 'contestant' signed up 'to save her marriage' by becoming more attractive to her husband. Every part of her, from her teeth down to her tummy, was reduced, enhanced or otherwise adjusted. Did it work? It certainly changed her appearance, but the next morning I imagine she was still the same person inside and, probably more to the point, so was her husband. That sort of change is only skin deep.

– there's far more to life when the light of God is restored to us'. In the words of Chris Tarrant on *Who Wants to Be a Millionaire?* 'We don't want to give you that!'

So chapter 2 of Ecclesiastes says that, yes, work can be hard. But work does have a satisfying meaning and eternal purpose when we see it as the gift of our heavenly father who made us to work for him (2:24). In chapter 3 the author says that, yes, time seems to march on in an endless circle of life and death. But, if there is a Creator, there is also a beginning and an end to creation, not just a pointless closed system.

Ecclesiastes 3:11 gives the highly significant piece of information that God has placed that sense of eternity and enduring significance in all people's hearts. The problem isn't that people need to be convinced that there's more to life than the daily grind. The problem is that people have buried the answer of God's eternity so deep that they cease to be able to fathom it any more.

Connecting with people is about reawakening in them a sense of eternity – reminding them that God has purposes that will endure forever (3:14), that our wickedness has caused the gap to form between us and the Creator Judge (3:16) and that God will bring all people to account (3:17; 12:13–14).

Ecclesiastes takes the lid off our culture, which lives as if the here and now 'under the sun' is all that matters. The challenge for the church is to connect people to the reality that our rejection of God is more than a little gap we can step over if we try hard enough, but a chasm which is impassable alone. The opportunity for the church is then to connect people to the reality of grace. God is the loving ruler of the world and, despite the fact that we have rejected him and deserve his judgement, he has paid to give us the life of forgiven friendship with himself.

The church says mind the gap and use the bridge.

Because Christ's church connects our culture to God's truth

When the Babylonians defeated Israel, they took the Jews into exile and aimed to assimilate them into their culture. Their plan is clearly laid out in Daniel 1:

Stage 1: Pick the culture brokers who influence others and get them young before their minds are made up (vv. 3–4)

Stage 2: Give them new names and identities (v. 7)

Stage 3: Choose a key man to oversee assimilation (v. 3)

Stage 4: Give them a taste of the good life (v. 5)

Stage 5: Put them on a three-year MBA programme (Masters in Babylonian Assimilation) (v. 5)

The king of Babylon was playing an extended game. He knew that the God-ward focus of the Israelites was very strong, so he committed years to breaking down their dependency on God piece by piece. But Daniel resolved to stand firm against the godless, secular values surrounding him. He associated with the Babylonians, but didn't allow himself to be assimilated into their culture and values. He knew the difference and he knew where to draw the line. For example, at an early stage he decided to take a stand by refusing to eat the king's food – not because the food was any more or less contaminated by pagan rituals than any other food (including the vegetables he did end up eating), but because he knew the power of mealtimes. He didn't want to be drawn in by the luxurious lifestyle or seductive power of sharing the king's table.

Daniel kept his devotion to God pure, but that didn't prevent him from taking an active part in Babylonian society and rising quickly in the ranks. Daniel was an effective witness to God precisely because he worked within the Babylonian culture and yet remained distinct from it. He held a position of influence within society from which he was willing to point people to the truth about God and their godless culture. For example, Daniel says to King Belshazzar:

'You have set yourself up against the Lord of heaven... You praised the gods of silver and gold, of bronze, iron, wood and stone, which cannot see or hear or understand. But you did not honour the God who holds in his hand your life and all your ways' (Dan. 5:23).

Daniel 1

3 Then the king ordered Ashpenaz, chief of his court officials, to bring in some of the Israelites from the royal family and the nobility – 4 young men without any physical defect, handsome, showing aptitude for every kind of learning, well informed, quick to understand, and qualified to serve in the king's palace. He was to teach them the language and literature of the Babylonians. 5 The king assigned them a daily amount of food and wine from the king's table. They were to be trained for three years, and after that they were to enter the king's service. 6 Among these were some from Judah: Daniel, Hananiah, Mishael and Azariah. 7 The chief official gave them new names: to Daniel, the name Belteshazzar; to Hananiah, Shadrach; to Mishael, Meshach; and to Azariah, Abednego.

8 But Daniel resolved not to defile himself with the royal food and wine, and he asked the chief official for permission not to defile himself in this way.

1 Peter 3

15 Always be prepared to give an answer to everyone who asks you to give the reason for the hope that you have. But do this with gentleness and respect.

Ney Bailey[7] tells the story of when she was Personnel Director for Campus Crusade for Christ and showed Bill Bright, Campus Crusade's founder, the results of a survey of 10,000 college students. He immediately saw the fact that over 95% said they wanted a more personal religious faith, but very few of them (5%) could give an adequate answer to the question 'how does one become a Christian?'

Ney Bailey describes how Bill Bright was 'gripped by the statistics' and simply said three times 'they don't know how', then 'suddenly he put his head down on his arms on his desk and sobbed for what seemed like a long time.'

She concludes: 'all these years I've remembered that holy moment. That, to me, revealed the heart of Bill Bright. And it was that heart of his which was like God's heart that influenced every decision he made in the subsequent years.'

In the same way, every decision a church makes needs to take on the challenge of being all things to all people in order to save some (1 Cor. 9:22) by connecting them to the only source of spiritual answers: Jesus, the way, the truth and the life.

Acts 17

22 'Men of Athens! I see that in every way you are very religious. 23 For as I walked around and looked carefully at your objects of worship, I even found an altar with this inscription: to an unknown god. Now what you worship as something unknown I am going to proclaim to you.'

Daniel connects the king to God by showing him the futility of praising lifeless idols and the gravity of rejecting the living God who sustains everything. That's the task of God's people in every generation: to be ready to give an answer for our distinct hope.

1 Peter 3 says that connecting with culture will involve the following:
1. Remaining set apart – without an intensity of light in our hearts we won't connect by bringing a contrast to the darkness –instead we will simply merge with it.
2. Speaking up for our distinctive hope.
3. Being in relationship – rather than just churning out truth claims, we are to respect the person we're speaking to and understand where they're coming from. Without compromising the light we are told to gently guide, not force, people to the light. The power is in the light – not in us.

Paul was a master connector. As we saw at the relationship building stage (Step 2), Paul doesn't just learn about a culture but lives a culture for a reason – to save some (1 Cor. 9:19–23). Paul practises incarnation for the sake of connection – gaining an opportunity to speak the pan-cultural message of Christ.

Paul's speech in Athens is an example of pointing people to Jesus by first establishing a point of connection with their culture:
1. Paul begins with the Athenians' concerns and practices, using observations on their religiousness and quotes from their poets.
2. He then highlights the inadequacy of trusting gods that humans make.
3. From there he points them to the truth of God, who is creator and judge of all.
Paul builds a bridge, starting with the darkness of their situation and leading them to the light of God's solution.

Because the gap is getting alarmingly wide
(The 'secular' barrier to relevance building)

The concept of living life 'under the sun' without God has been in existence since it was first coined by the writer of Ecclesiastes. But as concepts go it seems to have matured with age rather than withered.

It is almost a 'given' that our society is increasingly secular and 'post-Christian'. It is a difficult concept to substantiate since it requires us to measure devotion to God rather than simply church attendance. After all, throughout history there have been plenty of secular-hearted people who have attended churches; plenty of people who have said they were Christians when they didn't love Christ at all. What we can say is that the distinction between secular unbelievers and Christ worshippers is becoming increasingly clear. There's a much smaller middle ground of 'secular churchgoers'. People who don't want to go to church don't go to church. The gap between 'the churched' and 'the unchurched' is getting wider and wider. For many people, the issue isn't that church is boring – it just isn't an issue full stop. Christianity is irrelevant for a whole new generation because it's unknown, and it's unknown because it remains 'untried'.
'For every 100 children who were in Sunday school in 1930 (and who are now in their seventies or eighties), there are only 9 today.'[8]

Nick Spencer's group interviews with people who are neither convinced atheists nor definite believers in God[9] found that:

1. Being 'religious' is not seen as a good thing. Interviewees used the following words in talking about religion: 'hypocrisy...boring...scandalous...child abusers...conflicting... blinkered'.

2. Most disliked religion, but for some it was just old and irrelevant:
'I would agree that a lot of rules that were set out so many millions of years ago or whatever, they are not really relevant in today's society.'

'The story behind it all just doesn't interest me at all, it's just what I believe about here and now you know.'

3. People generally think that Christianity imposes too rigid a code. People want to feel proud of what they do and build a bespoke morality to fit their lifestyle.
Psalm 2 says that people 'gather together against the LORD and against his Anointed One. "Let us break their chains," they say, "and throw off their fetters."'
'I don't have to go round pretending that I am going to be holy as long as I'm good and kind to people, and basically look after, be good to my family.'
'If you were church[going] you are going to live by the church's morals, where they tell you what to do rather than thinking for yourself what is good or bad.'
'My choice is that church doesn't come into it, and I live my life as I believe I should live it, and make my decisions and hope they are good ones.'

4. People know very little about the Bible, but that didn't stop people from rejecting it. 'I don't know all the specifics of it.' 'I have never read the Bible from front to back.' 'It's like *Lord of the Rings*, isn't it? I mean it's all about another universe – a middle earth.' 'Is that part of the Bible then, *War and Peace?*' 'There's no evidence to support anything in the Bible.'

Lee Strobel[11] has identified some key characteristics of an unbeliever:
1. Rejected church but not necessarily God
2. Morally adrift but secretly wants an anchor
3. Resists rules but responds to reasons
4. Doesn't understand Christianity or even what he claims to believe in
5. Doesn't expect answers to questions from Christians
6. Asks 'Does it work?' before 'Is it true?'
7. Wants to experience something, not just know about it
8. Wants to be a friend, not a project.

Four yearnings of unbelievers:[12]
1. To feel understood
2. To understand
3. To belong
4. To have hope.

Michael Marshall points to the irrelevancy of commissioning focus groups who reach the blindingly obvious conclusion that the church is becoming increasingly irrelevant to young people or, as he says: '"Becoming?" – you must be joking!' He makes the point that we have our self-indulgent debates and 'in the meantime, as Milton said – "the sheep look up and are no longer fed," or as I'm often tempted to paraphrase it: "the sheep are fed up and no longer looking!"'[13]

So what?

People aren't reaching the conclusion that the good news of Christ is irrelevant because the gospel has lost its power for people, but because the power of the gospel is lost on people. People are so deceived that they see Christianity as having a lot to do with restrictive morality and very little to do with real life. As Callum Brown's analysis of Christianity in Britain concludes: 'what emerges is a story not merely of church decline, but the end of Christianity as a means by which men and women, as individuals, construct their identities and their sense of "self".'[10]
People have rejected the framework of Christian principles for so long that it's often difficult for people to understand what is talked about in churches without a remedial Christianity class. Christians need to be trained TCFL – Teaching Christianity as a Foreign Language.

We don't need to make the gospel message relevant – by its nature it is! What we do need to do is work at ways of connecting people with the gospel's relevance.

Abraham Maslow's hierarchy of needs helps us to see that, before the spiritual 'self actualization' need can be addressed, people need to feel comfortable, safe and then loved and valued. In the 1970's the Cognitive need of knowledge and meaning and the Aesthetic need of beauty, balance and form were added between the needs of Esteem and Self actualization. Since, the higher needs cannot generally be met until the ones below have been met, the hierarchy highlights the distance many are from being ready to think seriously about spiritual issues.

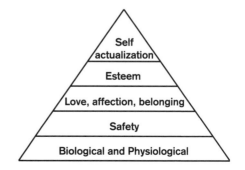

Step 1. Preparation.		Step 2. Relationship building.			Step 3. Respect building		
Strategy expertise	Strategy process	Isolated	Liquid	Multi choice	Weird	Insular	Hypocritical
Preparation solutions		Relationship building solutions			Respect building solutions		

Because people lack answers to their questions of life
(The 'uncertainty' barrier to relevance building)

A world of less certainty is also a world of more questions:

1. Deregulation
– Personal rights and 'being true to yourself' are all that matter.
– People live for the moment – 'carpe diem'.
– Institutions are irrelevant. Hierarchy is replaced by 'permission giving networks'. Leaders are no longer trusted.

2. Doubt everything
– The only truth is that there is no absolute truth.– People are less aware of Christianity. If you asked the average person in the UK, 'Would you like to come to my church?' they'd probably ask 'Why?'
– Distinctions are blurred between truth and error, right and wrong.
– Christianity seen as lifestyle choice, not universal truth.

3. Chaos
– The modern preoccupation with avoiding chaos has been replaced with a postmodern embracing of it.

4. Meaninglessness
– Where once there was a mechanistic confidence in cause and effect, there is postmodern angst of unrealized potentials.
– The Mall of America in Minneapolis attracts 40 million visitors a year – more than Disney World, Disneyland and the Grand Canyon combined.
– Choice and competition generate the illusion that everybody can have everything they want when they want. But it's an impossibility that leads to unreasonable demands on producers and unachievable goals for consumers.
'We are moving toward increasingly perfect markets. The result is total competition. In the surplus society the customer is more than king: the customer is the mother of all dictators.'[14]

'Control...has been tacitly transferred into the hands of tens of millions – soon to be hundreds of millions – of users worldwide.'[15]

'Freedom has been thrust back into our hands. Institutions used to work to create certainty. Now the certainties are withering. Blind loyalty has died... We shop around. Lifelong membership is defunct... We are more promiscuous about our institutions... Values used to be built around structures and clear expectations. Now, values are a moveable feast as our value systems are liberalised.'[16]

'Our society values sceptics who question everything over faithful people who trust. You can be as stupid as a cabbage as long as you doubt.'[17]

'We watch TV to figure out ourselves, to be reassured that we're better off, mentally, physically or financially, than the freaks on display.'[18]

'Liquid church involves a radical change in attitude for the church... Instead of opposing materialism and treating consumer choice as evil, we need to begin to embrace the sensibilities of consumption. This means that we must develop a church life that connects with what people want, and one vital ingredient will make this change possible. The church must change its emphasis from meeting people's spiritual needs to stimulating their desires.'[19]

'Women and men are no longer satisfied with the thesis, "I think therefore I am". They want to touch and taste, to hear and smell, to hold and to be held. They want a faith and a community of faith that embraces all the senses, not just the intellect. Unless we are willing to radically rethink how we "do" church in order to facilitate those relationships with God and with one another, there's little hope of satisfying the spiritual hunger of the gathered community of God, let alone attracting the spiritually hungry who experiment with a whole host of alternative forms of spirituality.'[21]

'It is vital that, as churches, we make room for the dark side, the down side, the desperate struggles of people in the teeth of life's dangers and difficulties. Sin means that our world is a messy, uncomfortable place. Faith helps us to live in that world; it does not lift us out of it.'[22]

'What is the church there for in our secular society? To give room for the questions which are common to everyone but only Christianity has a specific answer to. Our specific task is to give expression to Christian faith in a postmodern age. We should not ignore social action but must not forget to define our main task because nobody else will do that for us.'[23]

So what?

1. Connecting churches will maintain a call to repentance
The church survey 'Let the people speak':[20]
'People want churches to emphasise the many reasons why believing in God and Christianity makes sense and to challenge a doubting society... This subject [of apologetics] emerged as a fundamental reason why people were not being attracted to the church, being mentioned implicitly or explicitly in 73% of the letters received... Replies revealed frustration that unlike churches in other parts of the world, ministers in the British Isles often failed to confront scepticism with any meaningful challenge.'
'People want churches to give clear teaching on the nature of God's holiness... Approximately 75% of those responding... pointed out that while many believe in God, they regard him as undemanding and not requiring obedience or any particular standard of conduct... Therefore many people have no inclination to attend church and see no advantage or attraction in ever doing so.'
'Want churches to respond to the needs of this frightened generation by adopting a "visionary and prophetic role"... courageously condemn immorality and corruption.'

2. Connecting churches will give people freedom to explore faith and make informed 'choices' for themselves. Churches need to adapt to a move from lectures to sound-bites – people are less ready to listen to long talks. Discussion is key.

3. Connecting churches will build an organic network of people, not a mechanistic organization.People are attracted to a movement rather than an organization. As people choose friends based more on affinity than geography churches need to rely more on people being brought to church by friends rather than them walking in.

4. Connecting churches will be about a reality of mess as well as of hope.

5. Connecting churches will be about loyalty and life sharing in community. A church should reverse the trend that has turned students of life into consumers of lifestyles by turning selfish customers back into selfless servants.

6. Connecting churches will go beyond social action (respect building activities) into faith exploration (response building activities).

Because church services are seen as irrelevant
(The 'boring church' barrier to relevance building)

In an early *Mr Bean* sketch, Rowan Atkinson is at church – in a hard pew, attempting to sing strange hymns, hearing a sleep-inducing sermon as a mumbling 'blah blah blah' and suffering under a judgemental, unwelcoming churchwarden. The opposite but equally offensive TV caricature of church is found in every episode of the *Vicar of Dibley*, in which Dawn French seems to have no regard for teaching the truth of God as long as everyone's having a good time. Churches need to avoid both extremes. A reverence for God without a relevance to culture is completely inaccessible to many people. A relevance to culture without a reverence for God is completely unacceptable to our mighty Lord.

Nick Spencer's group interviews with people who are neither convinced atheists nor definite believers in God[24] found that:
1. People see church as dull.
'It's cold, and it's long, the sermon and it's not very inviting.'
'You sit on hard benches...they should have modernised it a long time ago.'

2. People don't think that church is a very effective service provider. It's not quick enough at reacting to 'customers.' 'The church should reflect what we want. The church should not dictate to us that you can get married, you can't get married. We want to get married. We are consumers of the church.'

So what?
In our consumerist culture it's no surprise that people want church to fit their requirements and meet their needs. Unbelievers reject church on the basis that it's not their 'cup of tea', wedding couples select a church that's 'a sight to see' and Christians shop around for a church that's full of 'people like me'. The challenge is to listen to what people would like without allowing them to set the theological agenda. For example, making the sermon shorter may enable people to get away quicker to lunch and shopping, but will it provide sufficient spiritual food? Baptising or marrying all may avoid rocking the boat in the community, but does it make a mockery of the vows?

In his article 'If You Can't Beat 'em' Dr Graeme Smith explains the process of inculturation. This is when we are influenced by beliefs 'from the pew' that are grounded only in experience. He writes:
'For example a church group wanted to produce a booklet about baptism for unchurched parents and godparents. They began with the usual stuff, the symbolism of water and light illustrating new birth in the family of the church. But further discussion revealed a different agenda: they wanted to say that their church was a friendly place, where people could feel comfortable – this was their theology of baptism. It was not an addition to the notion of new birth and the symbolism of light and water, but instead of it.'[25]

'The church both transcends culture and immerses itself in particular cultures. Here again, the church has trouble maintaining a balance. In its mainline forms the church has tended to value uniformity over particularity, universality over locality, cultural transcendence over cultural incarnation, and stability and predictability over innovation. Sometimes it has gone to the opposite extreme.'[27]

Martin Robinson observes how the British 'chapel culture' was established to meet the needs of a particular culture – but it has not moved with that culture: 'Visitors to such chapels can easily see the yawning chasm between what takes place in the culture of chapel life and the culture of those living in the neighbourhood. It is as if the chapel folk are silently saying to the community: "to become a Christian, you not only have to believe that Jesus Christ was the Son of God, that he died on a cross and was raised from the dead on the third day; you also have to find a way of living in a culture that no longer exists in everyday life."'[28]

'Making a service "comfortable" for the unchurched doesn't mean changing your theology. It means changing the environment.'[29]

'According to Pine and Gilmour, successful businesses will be those that market experiences which change people's lives.
And of course that's the business the church is in. For the past 2,000 years, far longer than any corporation today, the church has offered people the opportunity to have their lives transformed – by Jesus Christ...the very thing that our society craves is at the centre of the church's mission statement.'[30]

Style is helpful when it acts as a bridge of familiarity for people trying out a church community. An appropriate style enables people to access the unchanging theological principles of church without feeling uncomfortable or out of place for any other reason than the challenge of the counter-cultural gospel. Working on relevant styles is one of the 'all things' Paul is willing to be flexible on 'in order to save some' through the unchanging gospel (1 Cor. 9:22).

Research shows that people generally make up their minds about something like church within the first seven minutes. That's a challenging statistic. What impressions do people get during their first seven minutes on the church premises? Often the Christian members of the church either turn up late or are tearing around getting things ready. Visitors, on the other hand, often arrive five minutes early and can be greeted by a church of empty pews and / or rehearsing musicians. The first seven minutes of the actual service are equally important for impression setting. Does your service start with a 'wow' factor? Is there an excitement about meeting and an anticipation about connecting with God? With familiarity comes decreased sensitivity to the messages that our style of doing church projects. All churches have a style. What is that style? Is it what we intend? Is it appropriate to our audience?

The Council of Nicea in AD 325 declared that the church is one, holy, catholic and apostolic. But being one as an organized institution doesn't mean that individual churches won't vary considerably. Also, being catholic in the sense of being a universal church under the single head of the risen Lord Jesus doesn't mean that local gatherings of his body won't be distinct churches expressing a distinct local culture. Snyder and Runyon[26] suggest churches are made up of four complementary base pairs:

Organized Institution	Organic Movement
One (uniform)	Diverse (varied)
Holy (sacred)	Charismatic (giftedness)
Catholic (universal)	Local (contextual)
Apostolic (scriptural)	Prophetic (situational)

Solutions research

1. Understand the world we're connecting to.

In order to connect with the world of our friends, we need to understand that world.
– Read what they're reading (newspapers, magazines, books, websites).
– Listen to what they're listening to (radio, music) and watch what they're watching (TV, theatre, films, etc.).
– Observe the people they're influenced by (biographies, media interviews, etc.).
– Spend time with the people they're spending time with (accept invitations to parties, go out of our way to meet our friends' friends).

Talking to unbelievers is particularly important when you're preparing to give a talk or run an evangelistic group. Know what the issues are on the minds of people to whom you'll be speaking. Trying out some of your ideas with unbelievers before you speak is a great way of honing your material so it's engaging, relevant and understandable.

2. Build a connectivity profile

For each group of people identified in Study Guide 2:

a. General profile

What's their worldview and values?
– What is their attitude to politics, truth, institutions, etc.
– How do they use money and time?
– What do their possess and desire?
What influences them?
– What sort of music do they listen to?
– What TV programmes do they watch?
– What books do they read? What is their attitude to Christianity?

b. Spiritual profile

What are their felt needs – physical, educational, emotional?
How do they define their spiritual needs?
How do they fulfil their spiritual needs?
– What are their idols?
– How do they fulfil Maslow's top need of 'self-actualization'?
What's their attitude to Christianity as a source of spiritual connection?
– Are they 'returning seekers', 'disillusioned seekers', 'despairing seekers', 'deluded seekers', 'diverted seekers' (to alternative so-called spiritualities), 'non- seekers' (comfortable in their godless, materialistic lifestyle)?[31]

3. Research people's attitudes towards church as a 'community provider of spiritual services'.

Study Guide 3 included an analysis of the 'insular church' barrier. The analysis at that stage looked only at the misconceptions people had about the role of the church in the community. Further analysis is now necessary to clarify how favourably people view your church as a place they would go to in order to connect with God.

Questions to ask include:
– Do they see your church as a place of spiritual connection?
– What else do they think you stand for?
– What do they think you should be about?
– What's the quality of your contact ?
– What or who else attempts to serve their needs (Christian or non-Christian)?

How?
Conduct interviews in the streets where people live or work, or interview representative individuals or groups.

Solutions for individuals

Get training to know your answers
If we're going to connect the world of our friends to the truths of God we need to know those truths.

Always be prepared to give an answer to everyone who asks you to give the reason for the hope that you have. (1 Peter 3:15)

We can learn answers to common questions. See www.becauseapproach.com for suggestions of courses and other help on answering questions.

Pray for opportunities
The deeper our relationship with someone becomes, the more honest they will be about their feelings on life and the more opportunity we will have to build a conversation bridge from an issue concerning them to the hope we know in Christ. But we still need to pray that God will provide those opportunities each day, that he'll show us when they come and that he'll prod us into speaking out.

Know the strategy
Understand which events are appropriate to which friends. (See the final section for ideas on preparing and communicating an overall church evangelism strategy.) Pray for wisdom in discerning who to invite to what, for opportunities to invite them, for strength to make the invitation and for God's Holy Spirit to give them a willingness to accept the invitation.

Develop a gospel mindset on current issues
The more individuals regularly discuss with other Christians in small groups and other settings how the gospel impacts daily life, the easier they will find it to speak in similar ways with those who are not yet Christians.

Hold a connection party
Organize a party for friends and at an appropriate time (e.g. after the meal), introduce a speaker who can give a short talk on a subject of interest to your friends which connects Christian faith to the issues they face (e.g. parenting, a current affairs issue, a popular book or film, etc.). The speaker can then take questions and lead a discussion. Note: it's essential that friends know what they're coming to!

Use your story
One of the best ways of connecting with others is to use your story of how faith impacts you. People love to hear about other people and the reality of your story, warts and all, will always connect. You can tell your story in one-to-one conversations or during a connection event or service. Talks often leave people asking 'So what?' – your story can answer that question.

step 1. Preparation.		step 2. Relationship building.			step 3. Respect building.		
Strategy expertise	Strategy process	Isolated	Liquid	Multi choice	Weird	Insular	Hypocritical
Preparation solutions		Relationship building solutions			Respect building solutions		

Solutions for churches

1. Connection topical events
(knocking down the 'secular' barrier)

A. Connection events with a social element

These are good opportunities for people to 'taste' what Christian faith is really about and meet some other Christians in a neutral, relaxed setting. Such events usually have a focus that draws people to come. For example:
– A concert, comedy routine, film, etc.
– A meal and/or dancing
– A cultural activity such as wine tasting, or fitness and lifestyle events.
These are 'connection events' because they also include a point of spiritual connection which gives the audience a clearer idea of what Christianity is really about and why it is worth investigating further.
For example:
– A 'pause for thought' in a concert
– A talk or testimony after a meal
– A talk that relates the topic to the gospel
– A discussion of the film, play, book, etc.

B. Connection events with a teaching element

Courses or one-off events responding to 'felt needs' make excellent bridges from relationship building and respect building events to evangelistic courses. So, for example, you can quite naturally invite people at a toddler group to a parenting course, and then you can invite them to come to a daytime evangelistic course. Ideas for connection courses include:
– Parenting
– Marriage preparation
– Marriage building

One-off topical events might include:
– A talk on something like beauty, work-life balance or stress
– Viewing a film or play or reading a book with a message about contemporary life or other issues that can then be discussed
– A discussion of a current affairs issue.

2. Connection discussion events
(knocking down the 'uncertain' barrier)

Some people find that a less structured discussion group is a helpful stepping stone to a systematic gospel course. This can very naturally happen in a neutral venue such as a corner of a coffee shop or a room in a pub or someone's home.
There are several possible formats for discussion:
– An open question time and discussion with a facilitator
– A short talk on a big question (agreed in advance by participants) followed by discussion
– Bible studies on a topic such as Jesus' attitude to people; Jesus' leadership style; Jesus' parables; the Bible's attitude to work, rest and play; the Bible and science; the Bible's teaching on the value of people; the Bible's teaching on other religions, etc.
– Opening video teaching and/or testimony to generate discussion.
For more ideas on Bible studies and video discussion starters see www.becauseapproach.com.

You could also begin a reading group with friends who are not yet Christians. You will be able to give a Christian perspective on the books discussed – it's probably worth having at least one other Christian in the group for support.

Solutions for churches

3. Connection services
(knocking down the 'boring' barrier)

There are several elements to consider when designing a regular 'connection service' that will enable people to come and make connections between life and faith, including:

A. Invitation strategy
Will people come because a Christian friend invites them or because they're local and / or saw an advert? What sort of service would the people who you've made contact with (stage 1) and who have seen Christ in your conduct (stage 2) come to as stage 3 in their journey of faith? How will you invite them?

B. Pre-service experience
The 'just looking' option lets people come anonymously, just like a trip to the theatre: refreshments at the entrance to purchase or help yourself to, greeters at the door who offer bulletins and ushers who show people to seats but, otherwise, people are left alone.

The 'church community' option aims to engage people more and include them in the church family for the day: for example, a refreshment area where members can greet and meet new people beforehand and introduce them to others with whom they can sit (or not, if they sense they'd prefer to be left alone).

C. Service first impression
– Bulletins should be clear and welcoming to outsiders, not full of 'insider' language or strange-sounding events, pleas for money or crèche help or lists of personal congregational items for prayer, etc.
– Initial reassuring welcome from the service leader: assuming there are new people who don't know who the leader is, who aren't sure what's going to happen or what will be expected of them, etc.

D. Opening worship
– Are there elements of church that people unfamiliar with church might expect and/ or that might put people at their ease (e.g. singing a well-known hymn)?
– Are there refreshing new elements that will pleasantly surprise people (e.g. a video item to introduce the topic of the day)?
– Is there a sufficiently God-ward focus to the opening worship?
– Will the opening part of the service help people far from God start to connect with the reality of the living God (e.g. a solo song or reading that points people to an aspect of God's character or a prayer that demonstrates personal relationship with God)?

E. Style of music
– Does it (and does it need to) reflect the style of music they listen to (compared with radio stations they listen to)?
– Does it help people connect with God?
– Are the words you are expecting seekers to sing declarational or too intimate for them?
– Will you say it's OK for people just to listen if they'd prefer or don't feel ready to sing the words?

Step 1: Preparation		Step 2: Relationship building			Step 3: Respect building		
Strategy expertise	Strategy process	Isolated	Liquid	Multi choice	Weird	Insular	Hypocritical
Preparation solutions		Relationship building solutions			Respect building solutions		

F. Style of service

Heritage style
– Structured, reverent services with a familiar liturgy and traditional music.
– Preferred style of the generation born before 1945 but also of people retaining a heritage of churchgoing from childhood.
– Danger: People come out of sense of duty.
– Opportunity: A traditional style you can still communicate Christ's radical message.

Contemporary style
– Informal services with modern music and messages that satisfy felt needs.
– Preferred style of baby boomer generation born between 1945 and 1965.
– Danger: People come to have their needs met.
– Opportunity: Can encourage people to participate in community, not just fill a seat in the audience.

High-energy style
– A spiritual experience which moves and challenges people, with prophetic messages on real issues and high-energy music.
– Preferred style of some from 'generation x', born post-1965.
– Danger: People may resist authority and downlay Bible teaching from leaders.
– Opportunity: Can develop teaching that is high-energy and practically engages with God's word.

Relaxed-fit style
– A spiritual experience geared at a set of people facing similar issues which gives space to contemplate and relate faith to life.
– Preferred style of some from 'generation x', born post-1965.
– Danger: It may become an intellectual exercise and exclusive to 'people like us'.
– Opportunity: Can encourage counter-cultural lifestyles.

G. Level of participation

Passive crowd
People come and go to an event as an audience to a presentation.
Secular example: going to a film.
Seeker model: pure seeker service with mostly performance songs.
Believer model: cathedral with choir.

Participating crowd
People come and go as an audience to an event.
Secular example: crowd at a pop concert or sports game.
Seeker model: seeker service with worship that involves the congregation joining in.
Believer model: large church worship service where the sense of community is mostly found outside the service itself, in small groups.

Inclusive community
Everybody is welcomed into a community gathering to 'come and see'.
Secular example: village festival.
Seeker model: seeker-sensitive church service where everyone is included as part of the church family for the day.
Believer model: emphasis on being together as a church family and spending time afterwards to catch up.

Exclusive community
Everything is geared to one particular audience.
Secular example: members-only club.
Seeker model: seekers tolerated but nothing more.
Believer model: church geared for Christians and seen as 'a place for me' and my needs.

H. Use of multi-media

Projecting slides and video can fulfil a number of functions:
– They are clearer and more professional than OHP acetates
– They provide more creative opportunities to use colour picture backgrounds, illustrations, etc. (If they are done well and in such a way that they don't become a distraction.)
– Slide presentations of words and pictures during solo song items ensure that people can understand the words and help them engage with the meaning of the song
– Video clips in a talk can help illustrate a point, grab back people's attention and give the speaker a breather
– Vox pop video interviews can demonstrate how we're connecting the passage to what people really think.

The questions to ask before using multi-media include:
– Do you have the people to prepare the material and then to ensure a tight production during the service? (They need to run a rehearsal, produce running orders for the whole service and cue sheets for video clips, print out slides, etc.)
– Can you deliver the quality of slides and video that your audience is used to in, for example, their workplace?
– Will this media be a servant to the work of communicating the gospel or a hungry monster that saps the energy of the gospel workers by commanding a disproportionate amount of their time?

I. Style of preaching

1. In preparation, have in mind people from each of your 'target groups'. What will cynical Sally say to that? Will local Len understand that illustration? Will this message help uncertain Ursula make a commitment of faith? Will it challenge godly Gordon from God's word? We need to work hard at explaining God's word but always remember that we do so only in the power of God's Spirit.

2. Remove all jargon – never assume people know their way round the Bible or believe the basics.

3. Grab your audience with an introduction that relates the passage to issues they face and says 'this is why you should listen'.

4. Ensure that your content never leaves people with the impression that Christianity is about moralism – preach the grace of Christ every week.

5. Bring the message to a conclusion that relates the passage to people at different stages. For example, 'If you are just starting to investigate Christian things, then you might want to think about...'; 'If you're on the edge of faith this morning then your response may be...; 'If you've been a Christian for a while...'.

step 1. Preparation.		step 2. Relationship building.			step 3. R...p...building.		
Strategy expertise	Strategy process	Isolated	Liquid	Multi choice	Weird	Insular	Hypocritical
Preparation solutions		Relationship building solutions			Respect building solutions		

J. Discussion

Will you give people a chance to chat over coffee afterwards? Or in a more formal way through a group discussion slot during the service? Or in a question and answer session during or after the service? A question and answer session after the service in the main meeting space is less threatening for an unbeliever than going off to another room. To save people having to speak publicly, questions can be written down during a coffee break or put into the collection plate (if passed around after the talk). Post-service discussion allows unbelievers to apply the issues and ask questions relevant to them while Christians could go off to other rooms to apply the talk to their specific situations.

K. Making it real

Using testimony is a powerful way to help people connect the principles outlined by the 'professional preacher' with the issues faced by the 'ordinary pew filler'.

L. Overall

Leave people wanting more.
Leave people wishing they'd brought their unbelieving friends who face exactly what you've been talking about.
Run the service with the assumption that unbelievers have been invited and are present.

'Being seeker sensitive doesn't limit what you say, but it does affect how you say it.'[32]

4. Connecting with children

(Suggestions by Harriet Baughen, age 12)

That a church would have an inadequate children's programme should be an unimaginable thing. Unfortunately it is not, and many churches have not given enough thought to the children's group within their church. This part of the church needs to be structured with careful thought and time. There need to be responsible leaders who have been picked to relate with children in the church family and any more that might come in the future. There needs to be a good meeting place with space for a game or an activity and lots of little spaces which are comfy and calm for the small group Bible study. There needs to be a set structure to each lesson that should go something a bit like this: a game or an activity to get all of the energy out of the children, and then separate into small groups for a quiet Bible study. The lesson could maybe finish with a prayer where any of the children have an opportunity to pray. To give the children an incentive to pray you could have a prayer toy which you get to name as a group and during prayer times you pass the toy around and you get to hold the toy as you pray. The Bible study should be picked out carefully and you have to go through it before the lesson begins with the other leaders. The Bible study should be done in small groups of about five people; these should be made up of children of the same age. If children come that are visiting for one week and they are in a group and do not want to be separated then you should take these needs into consideration and not split them up or keep them with at least one person that they know. The leaders should be put with an age group that they enjoy and have experience of controlling and teaching.

Solutions for churches

5. Connecting through video

Early on at St James we did a series preaching through Luke. Each week we filmed 'vox pop' interviews with people on the street, asking questions related to that week's topic.

We began with a week on the reliability of Luke's Gospel and planned a service which defended the authenticity of the Bible. Our vox pop question was, 'Do you think the Bible is a special book?' We expected the answer 'No, because it's unreliable, etc.' But, to our surprise, everyone answered 'Yes' – they thought it was special. When asked why, they said things like 'because it's God's words' or 'it's stood the test of time'. But then, when we asked the question 'Do you read the Bible?' everyone replied 'No'. When asked why, they said 'because it's in a language I don't understand', or 'because it's not of interest to me', or 'because I'm not into big old dusty books'.

We changed the approach to our service that week when we saw the issue wasn't as much the accuracy of Luke as it was the relevance of such an old book – even one as special and highly regarded as the Bible.

Hints on producing vox pop interviews.
1. Use a digital camera (so the film can be edited on a computer).
2. People are more likely to stop if the interview looks professionally run:
– Have someone holding the mike / asking the questions as well as a person on camera
– Use a handheld mike and a camera that is substantial and professional looking (not broadcast quality, but neither should it be so small they can't really see it!).

3. Stop people with the words, 'Can I ask you a quick question? It won't take more than a few moments.' If they ask what it's for, explain you're from the local church and it will be played during the service on Sunday but don't offer that information if they don't ask as it may sway what they say.
4. Ensure you've got a short, clear and answerable question. If you ask two questions, make the first one general and the second more applied to Christian faith. (E.g. 'What brings you contentment? Does God provide any contentment for you?')
5. Keep the question the same for all interviews so that you can splice all the answers together later without having to repeat a question each time.
6. Be prepared to keep talking to people if they want to, but also be aware that if you've said it will only take a moment then you need to let people leave (and turn your 'bursting to reply to them' into prayer for them). It's useful to have a card inviting them to see the interview being screened, and gospel booklets to give out as appropriate.
7. Don't spend too long editing. All it needs is a title with music (copyright free) and then the answers one after the other. The only effects you will probably use are simple fades. A basic editing package (that renders footage as you go along) may therefore be quicker (and cheaper) and all that you'll need. Remember: it's the content that you want people to see, not your movie skills! For the latest recommendations on equipment, software and methods of projection, see www.becauseapproach.com.

Strategy expertise	Strategy process	Isolated	Liquid	Multi choice	Weird	Insular	Hypocritical

Preparation solutions	Relationship building solutions	Respect building solutions

Expert witness

Lee Strobel[33] started attending the 'seeker service' at Willow Creek church to write a story for the newspaper he worked on. He points to aspects of church that helped him engage and keep coming:

1. **Space:** People need to be able to come to church or a Christian event and be anonymous. Like the best shops, it should be OK to be 'just looking'. This is particularly relevant to our welcoming strategy: if people come and go and avoid our gaze we should allow them to.

The issue can be that Christians love the community aspect of church so much they fail to appreciate how threatening that can be to an outsider – unbelievers coming to church for the first time probably fear having to speak in public, may well be threatened if asked searching questions by people they don't know and often object to being put on a mailing list.

2. **Quality:** They are used to excellence in other spheres of life and the church shouldn't be the exception to the rule. Church can be enjoyable and exceed preconceived expectations.

3. **Reality:** If an unbeliever doesn't accept what's being said he should be able to see that the Christians not only accept it, but are changed by their faith. Honesty and integrity are powerful antidotes to a charge of hypocrisy.

4. **Relevant messages:**
 – Have intriguing titles and high user-value
 – Deal with 'why', not just 'what'
 – Are not holier-than-thou
 – Use everyday language
 – Answer questions asked
 – Delivered by speaker who seems to like me.

5. Engaging the senses: This is one of the points made by Michael Slaughter in his book Unlearning Church:[34]

'My greatest hunger, the greatest need in my life, is not to be busy; it is to be filled with the presence of God. If people don't recognise the spiritual emptiness in their lives, staying home and sleeping might do more good. God doesn't give frequent-pew-sitter points for coming to church. God can't design something new if it is still filled with the old. God wants us to start empty. We've got to lead our churches to turn to God's love first.'

'Seeker-sensitive services consist not simply of contemporary songs and creative drama but also of a preaching style that is highly relational and topical. It is extremely challenging to remain focused week after week on topics that engage the audience. This approach can all too easily degenerate into pop psychology or social commentary. People come wanting to hear from God. They want to engage with the Christian story. They want a message that is unavailable elsewhere. Preachers face the challenge of communicating the content of Scripture in such a way that the congregation hears it as a fresh word from God addressed to them.'[35]

Leonard Sweet[36] has developed the EPIC church for a postmodern generation:

Experiential – Postmoderns come to church asking 'is it real?' rather than 'is it true?' They want to 'live' truths before they embrace them.

Participatory – churches should be about people not programmes.

Interactive – learning needs more than just the mind engaged – multi-sensory.

Communal – the predominant culture people experience is one of 'communal anorexia.' – the longing to belong.

Interview with Nicky Gumbel, Vicar, Holy Trinity Brompton

What do you think are the main barriers to people investigating Christian faith?
Many people still assume Christianity is boring, irrelevant and untrue – that's been the case since I was first involved in Alpha in 1990. I find guests on Alpha are amazed when they go to church and discover that the music is contemporary, the message relevant and the experience stimulating, and they aren't constantly looking at their watch. People often have a kind of spiritual hunger – they feel a sense of dissatisfaction with their life. But they just think, 'That's how life is' or 'I'll try gardening or yoga or the gym or meditation as an answer.' They don't automatically turn to the church to find what they're looking for.

What helps total sceptics get to the point of attending and engaging with Alpha?
People often notice something different in a friend and then see the Alpha poster offering them an opportunity to explore the meaning of life. The combination of the two makes them say, 'That's what I want to do.' In my small group at the moment, one member already has five friends who want to come to the Alpha supper and no one in the group has had a negative reaction when talking to their friends about Alpha.
We find that people like courses – it is a culture that enjoys learning things. Some people come on the Marriage Course or Parenting Courses that we offer, and then it feels quite natural to go on to Alpha afterwards – some do it the other way round. Many are invited to an Alpha supper, which is basically a party to celebrate the end of the course, and they hear the short talk, see people like them, feel the atmosphere and it is quite a small step to sign up for the course. In the weeks running up to the start of Alpha, we often have a 'guest service' with a speaker that the congregation and their friends can easily identify with, and we include testimonies from one or two people who have just done Alpha. Daytime Alpha might have a morning event with a topical speaker before the next course. All these courses and events seem to act as a bridge for those who would like to come on Alpha but feel daunted by coming into an unfamiliar Christian environment.

How do you maintain connections with the worldview of unbelievers?
I'm always part of an Alpha small group. If I wasn't, I'd feel much less prepared to speak the next week. The average age on our Alpha is 25–27, so I try to be with that age range as much as I can – this is relatively easy as we have quite a young congregation. In the last 20 years, I have observed that the main issues people face have remained the same but the way they are framed by people has changed greatly.
I also read the main national newspapers each day, regularly play squash with non-churchgoers and talk a lot with friends and family, whose jobs and interests vary hugely from my own. I'll often run things past my children, who give me insights from the music they listen to, the films they see, the issues their friends discuss and their studies and ideas.

In your personal evangelism how do you raise the hope you have in Christ?
I just try to be myself when I'm chatting to people. Whoever we're talking to, we share a common humanity and that gives us a lot of common ground. Our worries and concerns are probably quite similar – and I try to be honest about these in conversation. I try to be genuine about my interest in people's lives and opinions and to be ready to answer any questions they have.

Study Guide 4.

Study Scripture Psalms 1 & 2; Daniel 5:18–28
How is the attitude of unbelievers to God described?
What's God's attitude to a 'bid for freedom' from him (Ps. 2:3)
What is God's warning to unconnected people?

Apply: How do these verses affect our concern for friends unconnected to God?

Study Scripture 1 Corinthians 9:19–23
What's important to Paul in sharing the gospel? How far is Paul willing to adapt to his audience? What does 'become like' mean and not mean?

Apply: What would you need to do and change to become more effective cross-cultural missionaries?

Study Scripture 1 Corinthians 14:1–4, 20–25
Paul explains that prophecy edifies others while speaking in tongues will not be understood by others. What is Paul's concern about how unbelievers will react to attending church gatherings?

Apply: What would your unbelieving friends think of your service? With what 'first impressions' does your church leave people? (To properly answer this you'll need to ask a new person to church.)

Relevance building.

SCRIPTURE

SETTING

SOLUTION

3

Analyse your setting
How prepared is your church to connect with people?
(See characteristics of a connecting church on page 109.)

Analyse the barriers to connecting with each 'Focus Group':

Secular barrier
– What is stopping them from connecting with a Christian worldview?
(See general and spiritual profiles on page 112.)

Focus group ....

Focus group ....

Focus group ....

Focus group ....

Uncertain barrier
– What questions are stopping them from exploring Christianity further?
– What are their objections to faith?

Focus group ....

Focus group ....

Focus group ....

Focus group ....

Boring church barrier
– What are their attitudes to your church as a place of connection?
– What are their alternatives to your church? (See attitudes to church on page 112.)

Focus group ....

Focus group ....

Focus group ....

Focus group ....

Relevance building solutions.

SCRIPTURE
SETTING
SOLUTION
3

Discuss and decide solutions

1. Values

How is Scripture driving your church's relevance building activities? 'We relate Christianity to daily life because Scripture says...'

2. Strategies

In the light of your analysis above of how prepared your church is to connect with people? What improvements could you make?

For each of your 'focus groups':
– What connection points can you make?
– What social connection activities will you develop?
– What topical connection activities will you develop?
– What discussion connection activities will you develop?

Focus group ....

Focus group ....

Focus group ....

Focus group ....

– What provision will you make for any of your services to be connection events? What changes would that involve?

3. Goals

What goals will you set for the coming year?

What goals will you set for the next five years?

1 *The Sound of Music* (Argyle Enterprises, Inc. and 20th Century Fox Film Corporation, 1965; video distribution: 20th Century Fox Home Entertainment, Inc., 2001).

2 Alec Motyer, *The Prophecy of Isaiah* (Leicester: Inter-Varsity Press, 1993).

3 *Moulin Rouge* (20th Century Fox Film Corporation, 2001; video distribution: 20th Century Fox Home Entertainment, Inc., 2002).

4 *The Matrix* (Village Roadshow Films (BVI) Ltd., 1999; video distribution: Warner Home Video (UK) Ltd.).

5 Details from www.samuel-beckett.net.

6 *About Schmidt* (New Line Productions, Inc., 2002; video distribution: Entertainment In Video).

7 Ney Bailey's letter to friends after Bill Bright's death in July 2003. Quoted with permission.

8 Bob Jackson, *Hope for the Church: Contemporary Strategies for Growth* (London: Church House Publishing, 2002).

9 Spencer, *Beyond Belief?*

10 Callum Brown, *The Death of Christian Britain* (London: Routledge, 2000).

11 Lee Strobel, *Inside the Mind of Unchurched Mary and Harry* (Grand Rapids: Zondervan, 1993).

12 Robert Randall, *What People Expect from Church* (Nashville: Abingdon Press, 1993).

13 Michael Marshall in the *Church of England Newspaper* (10 March 2000).

14 Kjell A. Nordström and Jonas Ridderstråle, *Funky Business* (Harlow: Person Education Limited, 2nd edn, 2002).

15 Quote from the CEO of IBM at an OECD (Organisation for Economic Co-operation and Development) conference in Ottawa, Canada in 1999 (*Fast Company* [January 1999]).

16 Nordström and Ridderstråle, *Funky Business*.

17 Dallas Willard, at an LICC conference in London.

18 Nordström and Ridderstråle, *Funky Business*.

19 Ward, *Liquid Church*.

20 'Let the People Speak' (Betchworth: The Ecumenical Research Committee, 2005) available to download at www.churchsurvey.co.uk.

21 Trish McLean, 'Contemporary Spirituality and the Church', *The Bible in Transmission*, The Bible Society (Autumn 2002).

22 Simon Jones, *Why Bother with Church?* (Leicester: Inter-Varsity Press, 2001).

23 Quoted by a Danish bishop during a Sion College study trip to Kopenhagen in 2003.

24 Spencer, *Beyond Belief?*

25 Graeme Smith, 'If You Can't Beat 'em', *Church Times* (8 March 2002).

26 Howard A. Snyder and Daniel V. Runyon, *Decoding the Church* (Grand Rapids: Baker Books, 2002).

27 Snyder and Runyon, *Decoding the Church*.

28 Martin Robinson, *A World Apart: Creating a Church for the Unchurched* (Tunbridge Wells: Monarch Publications, 1992).

29 Warren, *Purpose Driven Church*.

30 Michael Moynagh, *Changing World Changing Church* (Mill Hill, London: Monarch, 2001).

31 Eddie Gibbs and Ian Coffey, *Church Next: Quantum Changes in Christian Ministry* (Leicester: Inter-Varsity Press, 2001).

32 Warren, *Purpose Driven Church*.

33 Strobel, *Inside the Mind*.

34 Michael Slaughter with Warren Bird, *Unlearning Church: Just When You Thought You Had Leadership Figured Out!* (Loveland, CO: Group Publishing, 2002).

35 Gibbs and Coffey, *Church Next*.

36 Leonard Sweet, *Soul Tsunami* (Grand Rapids: Zondervan, 1999).

John 3:16
For God so loved the world
that he gave his one and only Son,
that whoever believes in him
shall not perish but have eternal life.

Luke 19:10
For the Son of Man came
to seek and to save what was lost.

5.

Response building.

'Because everyone needs rescuing.'

I am writing this on the day Marcia died. She knew she was dying, and just five days ago she got married because it mattered to Marcia that she made her commitment to her partner while she still could. Three weeks before that she had been in church to hear her banns read. It was the Sunday after Easter and I preached my heart out from the last chapter of John. As far as I was concerned she could have been the only person in the room as we looked at the risen Jesus saying quite clearly that he will return. We dwelt on the two implications of that statement for Christians:
1. Jesus lives in heaven, so when we die we will be with him.
2. One day Jesus will return and take us to live with him on the perfect new earth without tears, pain or cancer.
That message isn't just a lovely idea. It's a truth that mattered eternally for Marcia. We looked at John 20:31, that all who believe Jesus is the Christ may have life in his name. It mattered to Marcia that she received life through commitment to her Lord while she still could.

What gets you out of bed in the morning? Christians approach each day as people of destiny – knowing who they are and where they're going. Christians can also approach each day as an opportunity to change another person's destiny.

Jesus didn't just come as a teacher or a healer, he came to change the destiny of lost people. That's the issue in the film *Titanic*[1]. The ship has hit an iceberg, but it takes some convincing that there's a problem. The engineer who designed the *Titanic* explains the danger in the captain's office. He points to the plans and shows that with five compartments of the hull breached the ship will sink. Others still hold onto the mythological idea that the ship is unsinkable but the engineer replies: 'She's made of iron sir, I assure you she can and will it's a mathematical certainty.'

The church has a similar responsibility to warn people that they are in danger. When they say, 'But God thinks I'm OK, we need to reply, 'We have hearts full of sin, sir, I assure you without rescue we will face judgement, it's a spiritual certainty.' It's not always a popular message, but a person's

step 1. Preparation.		step 2. Relationship building.			step 3. Respect building.		
Strategy expertise	Strategy process	Isolated	Liquid	Multichoice	Weird	Insular	Hypocritical
Preparation solutions		Relationship building solutions			Respect building solutions		

Because Christianity is a life or death issue

It's amazing how concerned we can get about inconsequential things while we ignore what really matters – like when a footballer's haircut gets more column inches than an African famine, or when we remember to drive with the right style of sunglasses but forget to wear a seatbelt. In the film *Titanic,* Rose is warned that the ship is sinking and she should head for a lifeboat straight away. If she had said, 'maybe I'll think about it later, but right now I'd prefer to think about a nice cup of tea and a scone', we'd call her a fool. Yet that's precisely the 'can't think about it right now' attitude many people have towards Christianity. They are so busy trying to look good to others that they don't realize how they look to God. They are lost indeed without him – and not just in this life, but for eternity.

In 2 Corinthians 2 Paul reminds us that we have been sent by God as the fragrance of Christ (v. 14) to a world where there are only two types of people – those who are being saved and those who are perishing (v. 15); those who accept the message as life and those who reject it as death (v. 16). People often say to Christians something like, 'It's nice you have faith, but I'm not into that sort of thing.' If only they knew that what they are really saying is, 'It's nice you're being saved, but I'm happy perishing.'

Jesus has compassion on people not just because they are physically sick or even spiritually confused, but because they are perishing without God – facing the hell of eternal separation from the goodness and love of God. That's why Jesus weeps over the city of Jerusalem. He says, 'If only you'd known what would bring you peace with God'...if only you knew what horrific danger you're in and the fate that awaits those who reject God (Luke 19:41–44).

Luke 15
3 Then Jesus told them this parable: 4 'Suppose one of you has a hundred sheep and loses one of them. Does he not leave the ninety-nine in the open country and go after the lost sheep until he finds it? 5 And when he finds it, he joyfully puts it on his shoulders 6 and goes home. Then he calls his friends and neighbours together and says, 'Rejoice with me; I have found my lost sheep.' 7 I tell you that in the same way there will be more rejoicing in heaven over one sinner who repents than over ninety-nine righteous persons who do not need to repent.'

2 Corinthians 2
14 But thanks be to God, who always leads us in triumphal procession in Christ and through us spreads everywhere the fragrance of the knowledge of him.
15 For we are to God the aroma of Christ among those who are being saved and those who are perishing.
16 To the one we are the smell of death; to the other, the fragrance of life. And who is equal to such a task?
17 Unlike so many, we do not peddle the word of God for profit. On the contrary, in Christ we speak before God with sincerity, like men sent from God.

Mark 2
17 On hearing this, Jesus said to them, 'It is not the healthy who need a doctor, but the sick. I have not come to call the righteous, but sinners.'

There's a classic scene in the film *Terminator 2* in which Arnold Schwarzenegger, the good guy, has been sent through time to protect John Conner and his mum from harm. He finds her and simply says, 'Come with me if you want to live.' At first she doesn't know how to react, but when her son assures her, 'It's all right mum, he's here to help,' she starts to follow him to a place of safety.[2]
That's the message that should ring out from every church as well: 'Come with us and follow Jesus if you want to live – it's all right, he's here to help.'

It's easy to be lulled into a Disney-like attitude to life like that of Balloo, in *The Jungle Book,* who tells Mogli to just look for the 'bare necessities' and not to rush after things that can't be found. Similarly, Timon's philosophy in *The Lion King* is to banish worries for the rest of your days. But those are not songs that the people of God ever sing – they have a hope that can be found and they are worried that people might be separated from that hope for eternity.

'The Finding God wants humankind brought into a redemptive relationship to Jesus Christ, where, baptized in His Name, they become part of His Household.'[3]

That's why spiritual rescue work was always Jesus' priority – he said he came as a doctor (Mark 2:17). When a doctor knocks on your neighbour's door with her black bag in hand and stethoscope round her neck you know she hasn't come for tea and cake. She's come because your neighbour is ill – so ill that she is giving a house call. You also know that the doctor hasn't just come to say 'oh, dear' and offer sympathy. The doctor comes to sick people to make them better.

That's Jesus' vocation: he's the doctor who goes from village to village because he wants to offer the prescription to the fatal sickness of sin. That's the vocation churches join in, too: we're a medical team going from house to house and estate to estate and office to office because we want to offer the prescription that brings life with God. Just as Moses told the Israelites to look to the bronze snake lifted on a pole to receive healing from snake bites, we tell people to look to Jesus lifted on a cross to receive healing from our sickness, which is sin.

At a recent local history event we held at St James, the invited speaker showed some pictures of the Clerkenwell Medical Centre. It was designed by Berthold Lubetkin, who is famous for creating the penguin pool in Regent's Park Zoo. The centre is of special note because it was the first community health centre in the UK. But, as I pointed out later, in fact there's been a community health centre in Clerkenwell since 1100 – a church designed by Jesus, who's famous for creating life, the universe and everything.

Churches are spiritual medical centres in the heart of their communities, holding out the offer of lifesaving rescue to a world that is perishing. Why is it that so many churches seem to be getting out of the lifesaving business?

Because people who cling to worthless idols forfeit grace

There is nothing more exciting than being able to explain grace to someone who is exploring Christian faith and seeing the lights switching on. The wonder in their eyes is often followed by a slightly bewildered expression and the question: 'Why doesn't everyone know about the good news of grace?' Or 'Why have I not been told this before?' The answer is in 2 Corinthians, where Paul describes how 'the god of this age has blinded the minds of unbelievers' (2 Cor. 4:4). That's the problem we're up against – we don't just need to tell people the truth about Jesus, we also need to challenge their devotion to other so-called gods. As Paul says, even though he set forth the truth plainly (v. 3), they could not see the glorious light of Christ (v. 4) because their minds had been closed and their hearts shut off by a blind loyalty to something or someone else.

The Bible calls devotion to something other than the true God idolatry. When we love money or power or self, that is the idol we serve and are addicted to, and it takes the place of God. And, like any addiction, breaking it requires help from others – which is where the church comes in. Paul says that churches are ministers of the life-giving Holy Spirit (2 Cor. 3:6). Churches have a God-given ministry of idol busting – showing the futility of trusting dead idols and contrasting the life of trusting the living Lord Jesus.

Jonah 2:8 says, 'Those who cling to worthless idols forfeit the grace that could be theirs.' It's vital that we see idols for being the enemies that they are. Clinging onto idols isn't just a shame, it's fatal. Not only are they worthless as life preservers, but they also lead people away from clinging to the one true life preserver – Jesus Christ. Idol busting is an activity that can change a person's eternal destiny.

1 Thessalonians 1
1 Paul, Silas and Timothy,

To the church of the Thessalonians in God the Father and the Lord Jesus Christ:

Grace and peace to you.

2 We always thank God for all of you, mentioning you in our prayers. 3 We continually remember before our God and Father your work produced by faith, your labour prompted by love, and your endurance inspired by hope in our Lord Jesus Christ.
4 For we know, brothers loved by God, that he has chosen you, 5 because our gospel came to you not simply with words, but also with power, with the Holy Spirit and with deep conviction. You know how we lived among you for your sake. 6 You became imitators of us and of the Lord; in spite of severe suffering, you welcomed the message with the joy given by the Holy Spirit. 7 And so you became a model to all the believers in Macedonia and Achaia. 8 The Lord's message rang out from you not only in Macedonia and Achaia – your faith in God has become known everywhere. Therefore we do not need to say anything about it, 9 for they themselves report what kind of reception you gave us. They tell how you turned to God from idols to serve the living and true God, 10 and to wait for his Son from heaven, whom he raised from the dead – Jesus, who rescues us from the coming wrath.

I caught the bug for sharing my faith when I was asked to be part of a mission team from my church in London. I'd always been very reluctant to do something as frightening as evangelism, but on this occasion I said yes (mostly because the mission was in Paris!). And, yes, it was scary being sent off with another team member to a room full of intelligent atheists whose common link was their work at the OECD (Organisation for Economic Co-operation and Development). But that night changed my life because I saw that some people were interested to hear. I mumbled through my prepared talk based on John Chapman's book[4] but then, horror of horrors, one of the 'guests' interrupted me and said 'That sounds important. Could you explain a bit more?' And, as my nerves subsided slightly, I looked him in the eye and explained again the offence of sin and the forgiveness of the cross. After that day I didn't suddenly become a mini Billy Graham (not least because I'm taller than he is), but I did walk away from there knowing I could be part of something amazing – I could do what I'd done that night with my friends back home. I could tell them of the good news of Jesus as well, and some of them would listen.

That change of direction is what makes the story of the Thessalonians so exciting. In the few roller-coaster weeks that Paul was with them, they heard a message that changed them for eternity. As the end of chapter 1 says, they turned from clinging to worthless idols to not just knowing about Jesus, but to serving and trusting him as well (v. 9). They were rescued from facing God's wrath and instead began waiting for the new creation (v. 10).

The key elements of their gospel conversion in chapter 1 of 1 Thessalonians are as follows:
– They heard the gospel explained to them (v. 5; 2:1–6)
– They saw the gospel modelled to them (v. 5; 2:7–12)
– They received spiritual conviction through the Holy Spirit's work in them (v. 5; 2:13)
– They embraced the gospel with spiritual joy (v. 6)
– They changed their devotion from idols to God (v. 9)
– They lived a visibly new and distinct lifestyle in the light of the new eternity that now awaited them (vv. 3,7,10).

Evidently their conversion to Christianity was so radical that everywhere you went afterwards you'd find people retelling the story to others. Despite severe opposition from their own countrymen (2:14), and despite the briefest of crash courses in Christian basics from Paul, they still welcomed Jesus.

This story reminds us that the power is in the gospel's truth and in the Holy Spirit's work, not in our efforts. The Thessalonians' story also reminds us of the joy we receive from being involved in gospel work. Paul describes them as his glory and joy, both now and on the day Christ returns (2:19–20).

Is your church continuing to see the joy of people released from idols? Are you actively pursuing the ministry of idol busting?

133

step 1. Preparation.		step 2. Relationship building.			step 3. Respect building.		
Strategy expertise	Strategy process	Isolated	Liquid	Multichoice	Weird	Insular	Hypocritical
Preparation solutions		Relationship building solutions			Respect building solutions		

Because we are God's ambassadors of reconciliation

What's at the heart of Christianity? Friendship with God.

That's the good news of great joy that the angels announced at the birth of Jesus: peace between people on earth and God in the highest. I'm not a military man, but I do know that you only need peace if you've been at war with someone. That's true in all relationships. If I told you that my wife and I are at peace with each other again, you'd wonder what we had been arguing about. And we need to ask the same question regarding this announcement by the angels. If the birth of Jesus brings peace with God and his favour to us, what was the problem? I only need peace with God if I'm at war with God. Christ is news of the highest joy precisely because he solves a problem of the deepest sadness. So many people fail to see that their wrongdoing has made them enemies of God, and therefore they also fail to know the joy of being reconciled to God through Christ.

Bill Hybels often says that 'you've never locked eyes on a single human being that doesn't matter to God'. But I once heard Lee Strobel, a member of Bill Hybels' staff at the time, add that you've also never locked eyes on a single human being who doesn't face eternity without God unless they receive peace with him on earth. Both are true. Heaven is a tremendous gain and hell is a terrifying loss. Both are reasons why the ministry of reconciliation is such a vital task for the church.

In 2 Corinthians 5 Paul says that reconciliation:
1. Is something God does through Jesus – counting our sin against him and forsaking him rather than us (v. 19).
2. Is something God does through the church – we're Christ's ambassadors, imploring others on his behalf (v. 20).

Luke 2
13 Suddenly a great company of the heavenly host appeared with the angel, praising God and saying,
14 'Glory to God in the highest, and on earth peace to men on whom his favour rests.'

2 Corinthians 5
17 Therefore, if anyone is in Christ, he is a new creation; the old has gone, the new has come! 18 All this is from God, who reconciled us to himself through Christ and gave us the ministry of reconciliation: 19 that God was reconciling the world to himself in Christ, not counting men's sins against them. And he has committed to us the message of reconciliation. 20 We are therefore Christ's ambassadors, as though God were making his appeal through us. We implore you on Christ's behalf: Be reconciled to God. 21 God made him who had no sin to be sin for us, so that in him we might become the righteousness of God.

'The church is not the end result of the gospel by virtue of its existence; it exists so that the gospel can be carried out in mission to the world. The church is an agent of the work of the gospel...the church itself is apostolic in its life and purpose as it continues to give expression to the gospel... If the church should lose its orientation to the gospel as the reality of Christ's finished work of redemption, it would lose its apostolic character.'[5]

I love puddings – so much, in fact, that it would be a dream come true if I could open a dedicated pudding bar. It strikes me as a bit of a waste to go into a coffee shop to meet up with a friend and pay a huge amount for two lattes and a muesli-infested bun when for that money you could have a steaming bowl of rice pudding and a glass of water – just as sociable and twice as tasty!

But if I'm going to open my pudding bar (hopefully called 'Just Desserts'), I'm going to need to sort out:
˒ Position
If people are going to enjoy my puddings I need to be positioned in an area where people who might enjoy my puddings spend time – in the heart of the high street rather than tucked round the back out of sight.
˒ Product
Nobody is going to come into my pudding bar if the tables are dirty, the lights are dim, the waiters are grumpy and the puddings are covered in a thick skin and flies! The puddings need to be an attractive prospect and the pudding bar needs to be warm and welcoming.
˒ Publicity
My product is different from that offered by usual cafés, so I need to explain that to passers-by with clear signage and simple explanations of what it is they can purchase and why it is worth coming in to take a look.

In the same way, churches ready to spread the message of reconciliation will be places where people are, with an attractive product that people will want and publicity that people can understand.

Churches are rescue stations – at big gatherings, during individual conversations, in small groups and at evangelistic courses, we are ministers of reconciliation (v. 18), faithfully proclaiming the message of reconciliation committed to us by Christ (v. 19).

God could have declared his message of reconciliation in many different ways, but the one he chose was his church. We are God's gospel distribution channel, and our role is a vital one of explaining. As the Ethiopian eunuch asked Philip, 'How can I [understand this passage of Scripture I am reading] unless someone explains it to me?'

God loves the world, our communities, our families and our friends so much that he was willing to send his Son to die so that we might be reconciled to him for eternity. And God trusts his church so much that he was willing to commit to them the task of continuing as his reconciliation witnesses to the ends of the earth. Every Christian has stamped on his or her forehead: 'an ambassador of his Majesty, Jesus Christ, committed to spreading his gospel of love in the power of his Spirit'. Every church building is an embassy of God's kingdom in a foreign land. Every church gathering is a meeting of the King's ambassadors.

Now that's what I call a church worth being a part of!

Because people dismiss Jesus from their lives
(The 'identity of Jesus' barrier to response building)

The following are transcripts of answers given on camera during 'vox pop' interviews conducted outside St James Clerkenwell on a Friday evening.

Question: What is the truth about who Jesus was?

'I really wouldn't like to say.'

'I'd say a historical figure but not necessarily a sort of divine figure.'

'I think Jesus was probably the equivalent of a guerrilla leader. A kind of minor rebel – you might consider him a terrorist today.'

'I think he was a live person but I don't think he had any overpowering forces. I think he was just a normal prophet.'

'I think it's a parable actually. I don't think I know enough about it to comment really.'

Question: Does the truth about Jesus matter to you?
'Oh yes definitely, definitely, in the sense that I think any historical truth is interesting within its own remits and how that influences people subsequently.'

'Well some people believe that he was the Son of God and therefore what he said is somewhat important in their life.' [Question: What about for you?] 'Well I'm not a believer myself but I think the message is a reasonable enough one.'

'Well if you believe that he was really good and everything it doesn't matter if he was God.'

From *The Guardian*, 11 September 2004:
'What I do argue is that all faiths, particularly the embarrassingly dysfunctional Abrahamic family, have to acknowledge that no faith tradition is supreme, that no one has a monopoly on God or truth, and that the reality of pluralism discloses a theological obligation to be humble and self-critical, to pool resources, to work together for the good of humanity and the globe rather than fuel its blight and destruction.
If only we were able to assert a shared platform that transcended the platitudinous, to stand up for those who pervert our traditions, and to work together for justice that involves compromise and humility, we might even end up stemming the decline of faith in northern Europe. By demonstrating that religion still offers meaning, purpose and human values, rather than being at best an irrelevance or at worst a bloody disgrace.'[6]

One thousand randomly selected respondents in Great Britain were asked which of statement comes closest to their point of view?[7]
The responses were as follows:
– All religions offer a path to God (32%)
– What I believe in is the only path to God (9%)
– There's a way to God outside organized religion (33%)
– I don't believe in God (26%).

A 1977 survey of Australian students asked: 'What do you think about Jesus Christ?' They had to pick from a number of options ranging from 'founder of Christianity' and 'Son of God' to 'good man', with the final option being 'no opinion'. Nobody ticked that they had no opinion, yet only 6% of those surveyed had read a gospel since becoming students. The other 94% had formed an opinion about Jesus without looking at the facts.[8]

When I was fairly new at St James I went to a Willow Creek Association conference. Bill Hybels talked about how we needed to be a 'fully orbed church' involved in a full range of activities. I didn't disagree with any of it, but I knew we couldn't possibly do all of it. We were just starting out with a very small group of people passionate about building a church in Clerkenwell, but we were definitely not in need of more demands. So, at a lunchtime meeting, I explained our situation to Mr Hybels and asked his advice. I'll never forget what he said: 'Keep your focus on evangelism – put that on your front burner and add other activities when you can.' And that's what we did. For the first two years our activities were:
– A variety of community activities such as toddler groups, barn dances, football screenings, etc.
– An evangelistic course three times a year
– A Sunday morning service accessible to all
– A weekly midweek gathering for prayer, praise, teaching and training.

Question: What's the significance for you of Jesus dying on a cross?

'None to me. Nothing. Very little. Don't know how to answer that one.'

'There should be more and there's not enough. Not enough consciousness about the whole thing I imagine.'

'I think it's been turned into a false icon. People have ignored the fact of what the whole dying on the cross was for. They go to church, get forgiveness and think that's all they need to do.'

'If my ideals are friendship and doing a job that's important to me I don't think Jesus dying on a cross falls into that at all.'

[Sikh respondent] 'It's what brings people to Christianity. Like they say "Jesus died for you", so it has an impact on those he comes to.'

So what?
Respondents are quite happy to dismiss:
1. The identity of Jesus
'A guerrilla leader. Not a sort of divine figure.'
2. The mission of Jesus
'It doesn't matter if he was God.'
3. The call of Jesus
'I don't think Jesus dying on a cross falls into [what's important to me] at all.'

Strategy expertise	Strategy process	Isolated	Liquid	Multi choice	Weird	Insular	Hypocritical

Preparation solutions	Relationship building solutions	Respect building solutions

Because Jesus offers life in relationship with God, not a theory
(The 'mission of Jesus' barrier to response building)

I got one of those round robin 'joke' emails the other day entitled 'things that it took me 40 years to learn'. Number one was: 'There is a very fine line between "hobby" and "mental illness".' Number three was: 'You should never confuse your career with your life'; number four was: 'Nobody cares if you can't dance well. Just get up and dance.' But, coming in at a strikingly high number two, was: 'People who want to share their religious views with you almost never want you to share yours with them.'

People like to think that a conversation about faith is a negotiation between equals that will result in us meeting halfway or accepting each other's differing opinions. But the gospel is about Jesus, the only way, the absolute truth and the fullness of life.

The survey Gone but not Forgotten[9] found frustrations about churches being rigid 'teaching shops'. Some of the reasons those surveyed picked from a list most frequently for why they stopped going to church were:
᛫ I grew up and started making decisions on my own.
᛫ A questioning faith didn't seem acceptable to the church.
᛫ Many of the church's teachings were illogical or nonsensical. I became aware of alternative ways of thinking.
There was also a sense that church may have been more about teaching and less about commitment to that teaching in daily life. Other reasons that many in this group picked for why they stopped going to church were:
᛫ I never felt very committed to the church.
᛫ It was easy to drift in and out – my church didn't expect strong commitment.
᛫ My main motivations for going to church were not religious.
᛫ I believed that you do not need to go to church to be a Christian.

Nick Spencer's research concludes that:
'People want the church to move away from the command / didactic structure on which it is currently (perceived to be) based. It needs to be more about sharing, discussing, listening, informality, democracy and, of course, tolerance.'[10]

'Church leaving will have to do with Baby Busters' suspicion of easy answers; their scepticism towards "hype" and manipulation; their unwillingness to be treated as passive consumers; their hunger to have their senses satisfied; their desire to "be their own person", in their own style, rather than simply to follow the crowd or the dictates of denominational tradition.'[11]

We can easily communicate to people that we have it all sewn up.
As Simon Jones puts it:
'Life is a breeze. Jesus is the answer; now what's your question? Well, actually, don't ask questions; just believe what we say.'[12]

'People do not want to be processed in a propaganda machine; each person wants to be treated as an individual who is listened to, as a unique person whose opinion is respected and whose knowledge is weighed fairly.'[13]

The learning cycle

1. Receive information & analyse its significance

2. Reflect on meaning, discuss & apply

3. Review options & act

'The church has spent its time trying to convince people that they need God, while these same people busily seek spiritual experience... When people say that they are "spiritual but not religious" they identify themselves with a desire for God, but do not see the need to search for this within institutional religion. The reason for this by and large is that solid church has created an exclusive club out of Christian believing... The spiritual seeker sees the price tag attached to faith and looks for satisfaction elsewhere.'[14]

So what?

The challenge for churches is to provide an environment of discovery and learning about Jesus that doesn't leave the seeker with the impression that he or she is just a passive recipient of a prepackaged set of assertions.

One answer is to ensure that we have a customer-orientated, rather than a product-orientated, approach. Product orientation says, 'Here it is, take it or leave it.' Customer orientation says, 'How can I serve you?' This approach will mean more bespoke tailoring of our gospel explanation to where people are at.

It's vital that churches provide opportunities for spiritual seekers to explore faith without having to first sign up to a culture that's alien to them. The use of discussion groups in neutral venues will help, though the first hurdle is often communicating to the seeker that he or she can trust such activities as a place that genuinely encourages questioning and is non-judgemental.

In any activity inviting people to explore Christianity it's also vital that we take account of the learning cycle. The cycle begins with teaching information. People then need opportunities to reflect and apply what they learn through discussion and questioning. Long term learning is also assisted by providing for mentoring relationships that help people review and act in response to Christ's call.

For the many people not familiar with Christianity, a vital step on the journey to faith is gaining an insight into what a relationship with God looks like in practice. The more they see the nature of a life lived in relationship with God, the more they will want the same. The gospel isn't accepted because people are desperately demanding to know Christ, but because they get access to a supply of gospel information.

Churches can provide an insight into something that's received by faith – we can say 'come and see what the Lord has done for me' even if we can't say 'try it on and see if you like it before you buy it'!

Because people think they don't need anything from God
(The 'call of Jesus' barrier to response building)

Richard Lewis has developed the idea of cultural black holes.[15] Like cosmological black holes, they suck in light and emit none and thus blind us to reality. His examples include the American dream, French superiority and the British class system. Our society could be said to have evangelistic black holes – attitudes to God that remove the light of the gospel and blind people.

These black holes include:

1. The black hole of personal sin

One of the biggest issues people have with church and organized religion is the idea that they are going to be harangued for being miserable offenders. The book *Chocolat* by Joanne Harris portrays the perception people have that churches are full of hypocrites who are out to spoil any fun.

Francis Schaeffer was once asked what approach he would take if he had an hour on a plane with someone who didn't know Christ. He replied that he would spend the first 50 minutes convincing them that they have a problem and then the final 10 minutes explaining the solution. If we remove the problem of sin, we also remove the solution of the cross.

'My biggest problem isn't my sin, it's the attitude of a righteous God to my sin.'[16]

'If we talk exclusively of a God of love we baptise every aspect of their dysfunction. We also need to say "God hates sin".'[17]

2. The black hole of truth

Nick Spencer's interviews with people neither convinced atheists nor definite believers in God[18] found that:

1. Religion is about personal opinion, not absolute truth.
'If I ever have someone ask me, a stranger, my opinion on religion, I would say to them, I don't discuss religion with you, it's my belief as is yours, and please respect that.'
'If religious groups could respect each other's individual opinion.'
2. Christianity is not seen as based on truth.
'There is no evidence to support anything in the Bible.'
'Jesus was not a person. He's a made up character in the theatre.'

'Over the 1990s 1.6 million new people started attending church but 2.8 million stopped. Maybe this indicates that we can capture people's interest, even intrigue them – perhaps through Alpha or a seeker service – but we can't engage their long-term commitment.'[19]

'It seems harder for people to grasp the gospel than it is to catch hold of a snitch because we live in a culture where far more people can define what the imaginary snitch of Harry Potter is than can define what the true gospel of Christ is.'[20]

3. The black hole of commitment

When it comes to church, people seem to have increasingly low commitment thresholds.

4. The black hole of assurance

We must also understand that people are often deists – believing either in an absentee landlord who set things going and then doesn't get involved, or in a God who is clearly unloving since he let this painful thing happen.

But in the parable of the prodigal son, Jesus teaches us just how much we matter to God. God doesn't slam shut the door of heaven and give up on us. In the parable, the father responds to his son's faltering steps back to him by doing all the running and hugging and restoring. Justice would have involved sending the son away with the nothing he deserved. Mercy might have left him with the status of a low-ranking servant. But compassion gave him a restored relationship of love.

5. The black hole of grace

The concept of grace has been forgotten in a world of spin and religious good deeds:
– People don't think anything is free
– People are very suspicious of motives and agendas when offered grace
– People are often too proud to accept what they see as 'charity'
– Grace is largely untaught amongst children.

6. The black hole of tolerance

There was a Mayor of London ad in *The Londoner* in 2003 that said:
BELIEF
In Islam. In Christianity. In all Faiths. In Arsenal. In Spurs, Chelsea, West Ham, Charlton and Fulham. In PS2. In 95.8. In txt (safe). In holidays. In Father Christmas (maybe). In Mis-Teeq, Blue and Kylie. In salt 'n' vinegar. In pocket money. In MTV. In Zee TV. In denim. In Sven, Becks and Nasser. In Harry Potter. In Frodo Baggins. In the future. In friendship. In the most culturally diverse city on earth. In London.

Strategy expertise	Strategy process	Isolated	Liquid	Multichoice	Weird	Insular	Hypocritical

Preparation solutions	Relationship building solutions	Respect building solutions

Solutions for individuals

Rely on prayer

Ask to be a prayer partner to evangelism going on at your local church, place of work, etc. Find out specifics you can pray for and a way of receiving updates regularly. One great way to do this is to adopt a small group at an evangelistic course or stand-alone evangelistic group. Pray regularly for each member by name and request updates on the group and how you can pray.

Learn a gospel outline

a. Start with a prepared presentation such as the bridge diagram, 2 Ways to Live, etc.

b. Mould your presentation to cover the questions each individual is asking, not just the questions for which you have prepared answers.

'Sometimes too much is assumed in a gospel outline. The presentation doesn't start far enough back; it takes for granted that people believe in a personal God, the deity of Christ, life after death, and the existence of heaven and hell. There is the temptation to say too much at one time. We move ahead too rapidly for people to assimilate what we are saying. As a consequence, we are still speaking long after they have stopped listening.'[21]

c. Ensure your presentation challenges them to ask the three key questions about Jesus:

– Who is Jesus?
– Why did he come to earth, die and rise again?
– What does the message of Jesus mean for me in response?

Know gospel maths

Know the maths of how every Christian being involved in evangelism grows the kingdom exponentially in a way that a few specialists cannot – regardless of the number of people they speak to.

Live a gospel life

The more Christians see God working in their lives to change them, equip them and call them to works of service, the more they will expect God to work in their friends' lives as well. And the more the unbeliever's Christian friends are transformed by the gospel, the more clearly they will see a living relationship with Christ, rather than rule-bound moralism.

Conserve your gospel ammunition

There is a limit to how many times you can invite an unbelieving friend to the same or similar evangelistic event. It is also emotionally draining to invite friends to things and can introduce an element of awkwardness into the relationship if they keep on saying 'no'. Therefore we need to learn to be selective in whom we invite to what and when we invite them depending on their stage on the journey of faith. As we say at our church 'there are only a limited number of bullets in our invitation gun'.

It is worth having a friends evangelism action plan that we use in our daily prayers which keeps a note of what stage we think each of our friends is at and what would be the most appropriate event to pray towards inviting them to or what would be the most appropriate discussion of Christianity to pray towards having with them. (See www.becauseapproach.com for a downloadable personal evangelism plan.)

Solutions for churches

1. Understand the learning cycle

The three barriers to response reflect the three key questions in Mark's Gospel:[22]

Identity	Mission	Call
Who was Jesus? Mark 8:27-30	Why did Jesus come? Mark 8:31-33	What does Jesus require of his followers? Mark 8:34-38

Each stage engages with a part of the learning cycle:

Identity	Mission	Call
Review information Analyse its significance	Reflect on meaning Discuss & apply lessons	Review options Act

The variety of learning styles and the three stages of the learning cycle remind us of the need to provide a variety of learning opportunities so that people learn facts with their heads, understand principles with their hearts and accept Christ by his Spirit.

An evangelistic course or discussion group is therefore an ideal supplement to weekly seeker-friendly worship services and personal evangelism relationships. Weekly courses or groups enable people to discuss and question the gospel explanation they've heard in sermons. Systematic courses also ensure that people hear the whole gospel message in an ordered set of presentations.

Evangelistic courses provide a 'one stop shop' by knocking down all three barriers to response:

Identity	Mission	Call
Talk	Individual or group Bible study Group discussion	Epilogue at end of session Prayer in response to talk Weekend away One to one discussion

Step 1: Preparation | Step 2: Relationship building | Step 3: Respect building

Strategy expertise	Strategy process	Isolated	Liquid	Multi choice	Weird	Insular	Hypocritical

Preparation solutions	Relationship building solutions	Respect building solutions

Solutions for churches

2. Decide where an evangelistic course with a gospel response will fit into your process

An evangelistic course can be an entry-point activity or a follow-up activity for people already attending a church service or group.

Before studying the three options listed it is worth noting:
– No option is more right than another but one option will be more appropriate in a particular setting.
– The key is to choose one option and adapt each element of the process to fit an overall strategy.

A. Course first strategy:

This strategy puts the emphasis on an informal 'non-churchy' course as the most accessible activity for people starting to investigate Christian faith.

a. Invite your friends to an evangelistic supper event and/or 'guest' service at church where they will hear a connecting talk and be invited to attend an evangelistic course.

b. Make the course friendly, relaxed and focused on the needs of the outsider. During the course teach some Christian songs, particularly at the weekend away. Also demonstrate other aspects of church at the weekend such as prayer ministry and, on the Sunday evening when they get back from the weekend (or the Sunday after if they need a break), invite them to come and experience an ordinary church service (i.e. not a special guest service) for the first time.

c. Transition people from the midweek course to regular church attendance and membership in a small group.

Course first strategy

Relevance building events		Evangelistic course		Church service	➕	Small group
E.g. Guest supper & talk E.g. Guest service						

B. Church first strategy:

This strategy takes the view that an outward looking church service is an easier first event for people to come to and begin to look anonymously without the structure of a course.

a. Invite your friends to a weekly seeker-sensitive church service that connects people to God. In effect, church on this model is the 'shop window' – the entry point to other activities. It is deliberately 'non-churchy' and accessible to outsiders.

b. At the service, guests and the regular fringe of people who only come on Sundays are invited to take their faith further by joining an evangelistic course and/or by coming to a pre-course dinner to hear more about an evangelistic course.

c. During the course people see the gospel fair and square and are transitioned into small group membership by first experiencing and being part of a small group during the course.

C. Community group first strategy:

This strategy has the strength of people's existing network of friendships as its starting point.

a. Join up with other small group 'cells' and put on a regular 'community group' for your community of friends (community may be defined geographically according to where you live or socially by network).

b. Invite your friends to the 'community group' hosted in a local home or other friendly and accessible venue.

c. Start the event with a meal (potluck, informal buffet style so people can mingle).

d. Gather people for a relevant talk that connects with Christians and unbelievers. Perhaps add a solo song or piece of video, etc.

e. Invite people to stay for discussion in smaller groups.

f. End with prayer.

g. Once people begin coming regularly, invite them to an evangelistic course and then to join the whole church for 'celebration' services on a regular basis.

Church first strategy

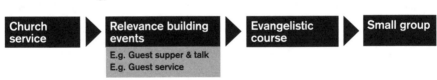

Community group first strategy

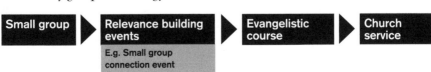

Solutions for churches

3. Encourage variety

A variety of non-course-based approaches will help prevent 'seeker fatigue' where an unbeliever has done the course(s) on offer at least twice and has a lot of head knowledge but needs to see a fresh perspective or link up with a Christian who will engage with him or her in a fresh way. Variety also stops Christians getting 'evangelism fatigue' by providing new and distinctive opportunities to invite friends and help them engage with the gospel.

4. Encourage discussion

In churches where the Sunday services are the entry point for unbelievers, it is important to provide opportunities for them to 'process' what they hear in the messages through discussion. Many people will do this by joining an evangelistic course, but for some that will be inconvenient or too intense.

If people are just coming to Sunday services, why not offer an evangelistic discussion group there and then? This group could meet beforehand (over breakfast), during (parallel with children's groups) or after.

For families, a group that meets during the service eases the issue of childcare. It's ideal when one adult in a family is not a believer and doesn't come to church regularly but is willing to talk informally with those in the church he has already met socially.

Non-course-based activities
knocking down the 3 barriers to response

Identity	Mission	Call
Guest service with gospel explanation.	Discussion of message in or after the service.	Response time in the service for prayer and commitment.
Talks at weekly services that apply each passage to the gospel of Jesus.	A testimony in a service relating the message to real life.	Invite seeker to join a small group or serving team where can see a Christian life modelled in relationships.
A video, short course or welcome event which gives newcomers an opportunity to hear the gospel explained from the outset.	A continuously running 'open to question' discussion group.	Link a seeker with a Christian 'mentor'.

Solutions for churches

5. Make a call to response at services

Response can be incorporated in all service styles:

A. Seeker-targeted service
– Everything focused on the spiritual need of the unbeliever, with a particular emphasis on showing the relevance of Christian faith to unbelievers.
– Opportunity for response by unbelievers: Even if primarily you are aiming to show the relevance of Christ, ensure on a regular basis you also show that knowing Christ as Lord is the most relevant message of them all. For example, if doing a more 'felt need' series, you could give a 'heart of the matter' talk on a regular basis (such as at the end of the series) that explains the complete gospel and gives a clear invitation to respond. This is especially important for people who have been coming for awhile but who have not done an evangelistic course and therefore may have heard bits of the gospel but not fitted it together as a whole.

B. Seeker-focused, believer-sensitive service
– The needs of the unbeliever are primarily in mind, but the Bible is explained and there is also corporate worship that will nourish Christians.
– Opportunity for response by unbelievers: Regular systematic preaching of the Bible will raise up a regular call to respond to what scripture says.

C. Believer-focused, seeker-sensitive service
– The needs of the believer are primarily in mind, but the Bible is explained and corporate worship occurs in a way that will also relate to an unbeliever and give him or her the freedom to explore without feeling like an outsider.
– Opportunity for response by unbelievers: Make a distinction in application between people at different stages of the journey. "If you are just starting to look at Christian things then your action point from today might be to..., if you're at the stage of knowing the claims of Jesus to be true but haven't yet accepted his grace personally then... and if you'd call yourself a Christian this morning then the application for you is...'

D. Believer-targeted service
– Everything in the service is designed to meet the spiritual needs of the Christian.
– Opportunity for response by unbelievers: it may be that a specific 'guest service' on a regular basis is more appropriate.

Solutions for churches

7. Train evangelists

A church that believes in every member ministry will want to have an every member evangelism training course. A passion for sharing the gospel starts with a compassion for the lost – something that is taught and caught.

Training evangelists should happen on several levels, starting with everyone and then specialising:
– A training course where everyone can learn more about the work of evangelism in daily life (see website for details of pre-prepared courses)
– Evangelism teams that give people the chance to pair up with another trained evangelist and see a gospel ambassador in practice
– Specific training and commissioning of members who have the gift of an evangelist are being called to use that gift to build up your church.

Running a mission series of events at another church is a very good way of training. It focuses the mind when in training sessions if you know you will be putting what you learn into practice in a few weeks time! Missions also enable people to develop their specific evangelism gifts in the supportive environment of a team, see others in action and learn the disciplines of prayer and preparation.

6. Preach for response

a. Understand your audience. Why has your audience not yet responded to the gospel? How can you adapt your approach (but not your message) to overcome their particular barriers to responding to the gospel?

b. Explain how a passage relates to Christ and therefore demands a whole life response.
As John Stott has said 'from the start people must see what they are getting into'. Underselling the cost of discipleship may store up problems when the going gets tough.

c. Use the opportunities given by the passage to uncover and 'smash' idols that are preventing people from responding.

d. Whenever possible, explain the problem of sin and the solution of grace as the context of rescue and response. In our therapy culture we can become relativistic about sin and see it as a condition preventing wholeness rather than an offence preventing relationship with a Holy God.
As Billy Graham has said 'the issue isn't getting people saved, it's getting them lost'.

e. Show what it means to live by grace, not works (recognize that your preaching of grace will often be misheard and need to be rooted in examples that make the principle into a more tangible reality).

f. Don't be afraid to confront people about the urgent need to submit to Christ as Lord (the apostles weren't!).

g. Be clear what the response looks like – give examples, use testimonies from others.

h. Give time for people to respond individually in prayer.

Expert witness

Interview with Rico Tice,
All Souls Church,
Langham Place, London

What do you think are the main barriers preventing people accepting Christ as their Lord?
2 Corinthians 4:4 explains that 'the god of this age has blinded the minds of unbelievers'. And I think this 'blindness' affects three key areas. First, there is blindness to Jesus' identity (he's merely a miracle-worker, a great teacher, a prophet or an example for us to follow, rather than being 'the image of the invisible God' (Col. 1:15), God in human form). Secondly, there is blindness to his mission (his death was a tragic waste, or merely an example of self-sacrifice, rather than being a sin-bearing, wrath-averting 'ransom for many', as Jesus himself puts it in Mark 8:34). Thirdly, there is blindness to – and rejection of – Jesus' call: 'If anyone would come after me, he must deny himself and take up his cross and follow me' (Mark 8:34). Those of us who are Christians know how glorious it is to know Christ, but many people have such a limited, low view of Christ – and such an exalted, high view of worldly pleasures – that they are not prepared to sacrifice one for the other.

What helps people move from interest in and understanding of Christianity to living faith in Christ?
The Bible says that 'faith comes from hearing the message' (Rom. 10:17) and that God's word will not return empty (Isa. 55:10–12). So the power to transform people resides in the word of God.

How do you build a call to response into your evangelistic speaking?
Billy Graham says that when he preaches he is concerned for the mind and the heart, but fundamentally he is addressing the will. That means we need to give people a clear understanding of how God's word applies to their lives, whether we're preaching to believers or unbelievers. And the call to response is not something that should feel tacked on at the end: if we're preaching faithfully from Scripture, everything we say should challenge our hearers to act.

In your personal evangelism, how do you keep a focus on a person's need to respond to Jesus as their Lord?
We must be praying regularly for those in our care – and most of all, we must be praying that they will recognize who Jesus is. For that to happen, we need to keep preaching Christ to them (2 Cor. 4:5) and trust God to open blind eyes (2 Cor. 4:6).

Study Guide 5.

Study Scripture 2 Corinthians 4:1 – 5:21
What are our motivations for evangelism?
What therefore must we do and say and not do and say?

SCRIPTURE

SETTING

SOLUTION

3

Apply: How will we become more compelled to tell others?

Study Scripture Acts 13:13–43; 14:8–18; 16:11–15; 17:16–33
How does Paul's approach vary?
What differences in the people and situations account for his changes of approach?

Apply: What do we need to be ready to adapt in our approach?

Study Scripture Romans 3:9–26; Ephesians 2:1–10
What are the key elements of the gospel we need to present to people? Is any of this optional or negotiable?

Apply: Do your evangelism courses and groups fully cover all of these elements? Has your church grasped the nature of grace and are you living the gospel out in such a way that people taking the courses can see it worked out in the Christians they meet?

Response building.

SCRIPTURE

SETTING

SOLUTION

3

Analyse your setting
Analyse the barriers that each of your 'Focus Groups' have
to accepting Jesus as their Lord:

The identity of Jesus barrier
– In what ways are they blind to who Jesus is and what he
means for them?

Focus group ....

Focus group ....

Focus group ....

Focus group ....

The mission of Jesus barrier
– What are the evangelistic 'black holes' that prevent them from seeing the truth of why
Jesus came and why they need his rescue?

Focus group ....

Focus group ....

Focus group ....

Focus group ....

The call of Jesus barrier
– What is the most appropriate learning style to help people move from information to
action?

Focus group ....

Focus group ....

Focus group ....

Focus group ....

– What idols are they clinging to in the place of commitment to Jesus as Lord?

Focus group ....

Focus group ....

Focus group ....

Focus group ....

Response building solutions.

SCRIPTURE
SETTING
SOLUTION 3

Discuss and decide solutions
1. Values
How is Scripture driving your church in evangelism?
'We explore the gospel with people because Scripture says...

2. Strategies
Will you adopt a church-first, course-first or community group-first strategy?

What combination of non-course-based learning and discussion opportunities will you offer?

What ideas will you adopt to encourage response to the gospel call at services?

How will you train evangelists?

3. Goals
What goals will you set for the coming year?

What goals will you set for the next five years?

[1] *Titanic* (20th Century Fox and Paramount Pictures, 1997; video distribution: 20th Century Fox Home Entertainment, Inc., 1998).

[2] *Terminator 2: Judgement Day* (Artisan Entertainment, 1991).

[3] Donald A. McGavran, *Understanding Church Growth* (Grand Rapids: Eerdmans, 1970).

[4] John Chapman, *Know and Tell the Gospel* (London: The Good Book Company, 2nd edn, 1998).

[5] Ray S. Anderson, *Minding God's Business* (Grand Rapids: Eerdmans, 1986).

[6] Tony Bayfield, 'Religion is a Bloody Disgrace', *The Guardian* (11 September 2004).

[7] The Opinion Research Business (ORB) BBC 'Soul of Britain' Questionnaire: 1,000 randomly selected telephone interviews in Great Britain, 25 April – 7 May 2000.

[8] Conversation with John Chapman, Moore College, Sydney, Australia.

[9] Richter and Francis, *Gone but not Forgotten*.

[10] Spencer, *Beyond Belief?*

[11] Richter and Francis, *Gone but not Forgotten*.

[12] Jones, *Why Bother?*

[13] Gibbs and Coffey, *Church Next*.

[14] Ward, *Liquid Church*.

[15] Richard D. Lewis, *The Cultural Imperative: Global Trends in the 21st Century* (Yarmouth, ME: Intercultural Press, 2002).

[16] Wallace Benn at NEAC4 (Blackpool, September 2003).

[17] Bill Hybels at Willow Creek Association conference (Birmingham, 1999).

[18] Spencer, *Beyond Belief?*

[19] Jones, *Why Bother?*

[20] Based on an idea by Rupert Charkham.

[21] Gibbs and Coffey, *Church Next*.

[22] Rico Tice, *Christianity Explored Study Guide: Leader's Edition*, (London: The Good Book Company, 2nd edn, 2005).

2 Corinthians 5:14-15
For Christ's love compels us,
because we are convinced
that one died for all,
and therefore all died.
And he died for all,
that those who live
should no longer live for themselves
but for him who died for them
and was raised again.

Participation.

'Because Christ's love compels us.'

I once met a senior person in the Church of England at a party. We chatted briefly and he said, 'You must come over to my office in Westminster as I'd like to ask you more questions over a spot of lunch.' I dutifully called his secretary to make an appointment and was told that the only time he could see me was mid-morning in two months' time. I was a bit disappointed to miss out on free pudding, but on the appointed day I turned up at his office and was shown in. After the initial pleasantries it became quite obvious that he didn't have any idea why I was there, and therefore we engaged in aimless conversation, asking each other slightly vague and pointless questions until enough time had passed for him to politely call the meeting over. Without purpose, meeting together can be frustrating as well as fruitless. Church should never leave anyone with that impression.

Throughout the Because Approach we have asked the question 'Why?' Why do we do this activity? Why don't we do that activity? Why are we pouring so much energy into this? Why are you asking me to commit time, money and effort to those activities? Why 'must' we do it? Why do we do it like this? Why have we always done it like that? We've asked 'Why?' because clear communication of the vision leads to active participation in the vision. When we know the intention behind an activity we'll gain the motivation for it. We will be doing things because we've caught a clear vision for them rather than just doing them because we were asked to.

Church is a group of people who know who they are, where they're heading and what they're about:
– We're not just a random group of people who happen to be travelling together because we're God's dearly loved people.
– We're not just going on an aimless drive down roads that lead to nowhere in particular because we're heading home.
– We're not just playing pointless games to pass the time till we get to our destination because 'we are God's workmanship, created in Christ Jesus to do good works, which God prepared in advance for us to do' (Eph. 2:10).
We're a future-oriented church that shares good news of the future with others and lives life by the rules of the future

Because Christ loves and builds his church

Jesus loves his church. In love he gave his life to pay for his church to be a holy, blameless and radiant bride (Eph. 5:25–32). In love he builds his church and provides all we need to live fruitful lives (Matt. 16:18; John 15:5; 17:26).

I love church. I love the fact that I can be part of a group of people who are loved by God and love each other unconditionally.

I love the experience of going anywhere in the world and finding other Christians and being church with them.

I love the way churches are all the same at their core and yet very different in their packaging – from 'Disney style' churches with landscaped campuses and state-of-the-art auditoriums to our partner church in Mozambique with its roofless mud floor meeting space.

I love the earth-shattering potential churches have to make an eternal difference as Jesus' network of 'change powerhouses'.

I love the history of church, carrying out the same God-given mandate and activities from year one of creation until now.

I love the promise that church growth depends on God, not us.

I love the eternal significance of church as a gathering of people making their way together to God's new creation.

McDonalds use the slogan 'I'm lovin' it' – and if McDonalds can say that, how much more should Christians?

My aim is to encourage others to start loving it too. Whenever I meet someone in London who isn't going to a church I say, 'Why not come to St James at 11 a.m. next Sunday? I guarantee you'll find it engaging and relevant and that you'll enjoy the experience.' If they say 'OK, I might do that,' I then make doubly sure we've prepared a relevant message and pray doubly hard that they come with a readiness to hear God's message for them.

Ephesians 5
25 Husbands, love your wives, just as Christ loved the church and gave himself up for her 26 to make her holy, cleansing her by the washing with water through the word, 27 and to present her to himself as a radiant church, without stain or wrinkle or any other blemish, but holy and blameless. 28 In this same way, husbands ought to love their wives as their own bodies. He who loves his wife loves himself. 29 After all, no-one ever hated his own body, but he feeds and cares for it, just as Christ does the church – 30 for we are members of his body.

John 17
25 'Righteous Father, though the world does not know you, I know you, and they know that you have sent me. 26 I have made you known to them, and will continue to make you known in order that the love you have for me may be in them and that I myself may be in them.'

Matthew 16
18 'And I tell you that you are Peter, and on this rock I will build my church, and the gates of Hades will not overcome it.'

step 4. Relevance building.   step 5: Response building.   step 6. Participation.

| Secular | Uncertain | Boring | Identity | Mission | Call |

Relevance building solutions   Response building solutions

I recently had the scary experience of looking after a friend's dog while the family was away. The dog, called Holly, was very old and arthritic and didn't move much and I was afraid she might die on my watch. I was so afraid of this, in fact, that I kept getting up in the night to check she was still breathing. She slept in the bathroom and, so as not to give her a death-inducing heart attack by switching the light on, I would creep up close and see if there were any signs of her breathing.

Many people see church like that – as an old dog with barely any sign of life. There's a legal term which describes certain people as having a 'settled fixed hopeless expectation of death'. It might be a term to describe the attitude of some churches today. But church is the body of Christ and a temple of the Holy Spirit (1 Cor. 3) – the church of Christ will never die.

I once shared with some local clergy my aim of inviting everyone I meet to St James on Sunday. One person replied, 'I'd never invite someone to my church. In fact, I wouldn't go if I wasn't paid to!'

It seems we've lost confidence that church can be grown. But Christ says, 'I will build my church' (Matt. 16:18). – I don't think you can get a better house building guarantee than that – even Hades protection is covered!

It also seems we've lost confidence that church can be fun. But Christ says, 'I will be with my church'. His prayer for the church is that 'I myself may be in them' (John 17:26). – I can't think of a more fun way of spending my Sunday morning than meeting with Jesus and his people!

Church doesn't become dull with the passing of time or change its substance with the winds of fashion. It's about offering a menu as fresh and nutritious as the day the world was made – and millions of people across the globe still say, with Jesus, 'We're loving it!'

Helping us say that and helping us help others say that is what the Because Approach is all about.

159

Because biblical vision compels Christ's church

A classic business school exam question goes like this: 'How do you get a group from a tiny island that they've never left to a mainland that they are unaware of?' Most people's answers involve drawing a map and giving the group instructions on how to build and operate a boat of some description. But the best boat in the world and the clearest charts possible won't be of any value if the islanders don't want to use them. Before they'll get involved in the journey they've got to get excited about making the journey. They need to be captivated by exotic tales of all that awaits them on the far-off mainland. Their hearts need to be engaged by the destination before their minds will get engaged in boat building.

God's people have the most amazing destination – Eden restored. The Bible starts by describing our beginning as a place of beauty where all is pleasing to the eye, a place of relationship with God and each other and a place of responsibility without drudgery. Throughout the Bible we are promised that 'in the beginning' will one day be our new beginning – the day when we will again be with God in a place without death or pain or tears.

The whole Bible is the story of God making and then restoring a people.
– In the beginning, God the Father, Son and Holy Spirit said, 'Let us make church – a people in our image with whom we will live in loving relationship, just as we live in perfect unity.'
– God's first command to his people was to increase. God has always been in the business of church growth!
– But people kicked against church even then. Adam and Eve said 'No' to God. They said they didn't just want to be the people of God, they wanted to be God. They rejected God's rule and, as a result, quickly found themselves hiding from God and out of relationship with him.
– The rest of the Bible tells the amazing story of how God calls a people to be his church again. Jesus died so that we

Revelation 21
1 Then I saw a new heaven and a new earth, for the first heaven and the first earth had passed away, and there was no longer any sea. 2 I saw the Holy City, the new Jerusalem, coming down out of heaven from God, prepared as a bride beautifully dressed for her husband. 3 And I heard a loud voice from the throne saying, 'Now the dwelling of God is with men, and he will live with them. They will be his people, and God himself will be with them and be their God. 4 He will wipe every tear from their eyes. There will be no more death or mourning or crying or pain, for the old order of things has passed away.'

Philippians 3
10 I want to know Christ and the power of his resurrection and the fellowship of sharing in his sufferings, becoming like him in his death, 11 and so, somehow, to attain to the resurrection from the dead. 12 Not that I have already obtained all this, or have already been made perfect, but I press on to take hold of that for which Christ Jesus took hold of me. 13 Brothers, I do not consider myself yet to have taken hold of it. But one thing I do: Forgetting what is behind and straining towards what is ahead, 14 I press on towards the goal to win the prize for which God has called me heavenwards in Christ Jesus.

When I was younger, for some bizarre reason I was very keen on collecting miniature figures of composers from cereal packets. Mum wouldn't let me buy an unlimited number of boxes, so I had to eat my way through box after box and ended up with three Beethovens before I finally got a Mozart to finish off the collection. It's all changed now, though. These days cereal companies will send you the full set of whatever their latest offer is if you send them some money. The art of waiting is being lost.

A friend of mine has the theory that supporting a football team should be compulsory for children, because it's the only activity left that teaches you about patience and loyalty.

But church has a major advantage over supporting a football team – it has a final end point in sight. Football is played in seasons, and at the end of one year the league champions start again with zero points and the cup winners have to give their cup back and enter the competition all over again. Football is an endless cycle of competitions and seasons that never reach a final conclusion: a club that wins every cup doesn't retire from competition. But the prize Christians win isn't just a medal to hang on a wall, it's a place we hang out in for eternity with the Lord of all!

The question is whether we are anticipating that prize. Is the church practising the art of waiting for the inheritance kept in heaven, or is it simply about short-term experience in the here and now?

could be called out of the rebellious world of separation and back into the church of redeemed people.

Everything a church does should be carried out in the light of knowing we're heading for Eden restored, where we'll be God's people for eternity. One amazing picture the Bible gives of what the church will one day be is the image of a bride beautifully dressed for Christ, her husband (Rev. 21).

Imagine the scene. The groom is waiting at the front of the church when the organ strikes up with a fanfare. The church doors swing open, and he looks down the aisle to see his bride coming towards him in a sparkling white dress and an adoring smile. What is he thinking at that point? 'Wow! That's the woman I love and want to spend my life caring for, and I am so glad she's marrying me.' Revelation 21 says that's how Christ will one day see us. In fact, every day we're closer to the place where there will be no more tears or pain and where we will be in the fullness of fellowship with God for evermore.

Church is God's perfect intention, not some sort of necessary mechanism for keeping us in check. Church is about people on the way home. That's what motivated the Apostle Paul. He said, 'for me to live is Christ, to die is gain' (Phil. 1:21). He saw life as a race to the prize of being with Christ (Phil. 3:14) – a prize that Peter reminds the church is an inheritance that can never perish, spoil or fade – kept in heaven for you (1 Pet. 1:4).

Gathering as church should always be electric – it should be a taster of heaven, a home from home. The idea of being in a room with a whole bunch of people called to freedom from the slavery of sin and heading for the reality of home with Jesus should give us goose bumps.

step 1. Preparation.		step 2. Relationship building.			step 3. Respect building.		
Strategy expertise	Strategy process	Isolated	Liquid	Multi choice	Weird	Insular	Hypocritical
Preparation solutions		Relationship building solutions			Respect building solutions		

Because we're compelled to have a vision for rescue

At a conference recently a man came up to me and said, 'You probably won't remember me, but I was in your Alpha small group in Battersea and since then I've made a commitment to Christ and married a Christian and we're very involved in our local church. I just wanted to say thank you.' I can tell you, that made my year! I spent the rest of the day walking on a cloud. There's nothing more exciting than seeing the miracle of new life.

Jesus shares in that joy:

'In the same way, I tell you, there is rejoicing in the presence of the angels of God over one sinner who repents.' (Luke 15:10)

But what happens when the church starts to get 'evangelism fatigue'? Jonah was a reluctant evangelist. He knew how and why – he knew that God was full of mercy (4:2), and that everyone needs to turn to God in repentance (ch. 3). Jonah's problem was that he just didn't want to do it. He didn't have the heart for seeing the Ninevites turn to God and receive forgiveness. That's why he's so angry when they turn to God and he forgives them. Jonah had limits – he had placed limits on who he thought deserved to receive God's love. He was happy being a prophet amongst his fellow countrymen in his own backyard, but he didn't have the heart to go to Nineveh. In fact, he'd rather have gone anywhere but there. Nineveh was the capital city of Israel's arch-enemies. Jonah just couldn't bring himself to warn the Ninevites because he hated the thought that they might heed the warning, ask for God's forgiveness and receive it. Jonah knew God would relent from sending the calamity of his judgement on those who turned to him, but he still wished he wouldn't. There's a missing link between Jonah's head and his heart. The book of Jonah ends with a question by God that's at the heart of our concern for evangelism:

'But Nineveh has more than a hundred and twenty thousand people who cannot tell their right hand from their left, and many cattle as well. Should I not be concerned about that great city?' (Jonah 4:11)

Jonah 3
4 On the first day, Jonah started into the city. He proclaimed: 'Forty more days and Nineveh will be overturned.'
6 When the news reached the king of Nineveh, he rose from his throne, took off his royal robes, covered himself with sackcloth and sat down in the dust. 7 Then he issued a proclamation in Nineveh:
'By the decree of the king and his nobles: Do not let any man or beast, herd or flock, taste anything; do not let them eat or drink. 8 But let man and beast be covered with sackcloth. Let everyone call urgently on God. Let them give up their evil ways and their violence. 9 Who knows? God may yet relent and with compassion turn from his fierce anger so that we will not perish.'
10 When God saw what they did and how they turned from their evil ways, he had compassion and did not bring upon them the destruction he had threatened.

Jonah 4
1 But Jonah was greatly displeased and became angry. 2 He prayed to the LORD, 'O LORD, is this not what I said when I was still at home? That is why I was so quick to flee to Tarshish. I knew that you are a gracious and compassionate God, slow to anger and abounding in love, a God who relents from sending calamity. 3 Now, O LORD, take away my life, for it is better for me to die than to live.' 4 But the LORD replied, 'Have you any right to be angry?'

I once heard the evangelist J John talk about a time he was on an aeroplane in the days when films were shown on a big screen. On this particular flight they were showing *Apollo 13* (not an especially suitable subject for nervous flyers, I'd have thought). When the astronauts are stuck in space, the film shows clips of people avidly watching the TV news in countries all around the world – the UK, Russia, India, China and so on. These clips show how the whole world is holding its breath to see if the astronauts are rescued. At this point J John began to cry, and a member of the cabin staff came over to him and said, 'It's OK sir, they get back safely.' J John replied, 'Oh, I know that. I'm upset because people across the world are so concerned about three people stuck in space, they don't realise they face a far greater problem of being stuck without God for eternity.'[1] I love that story because it reveals an evangelist's heart – a heart of urgency to tell lost people about the desperate predicament of their sin.

'It's not the church of God that needs a mission, it's the mission of God that needs a church.'[2]

God has every right to be angry at us, but he is slow to anger and quick to offer forgiveness. That's the message we are called to deliver to others. Whether we think they deserve forgiveness or not, God died to give it to them. Jonah found that hard to swallow – do we? Does Christ's love compel us? If we are convinced that Christ died for all, why are we sometimes less than convinced that we need to tell that message to all?

Peter gives an outward-looking purpose for the whole church of Christ:
But you are a chosen people, a royal priesthood, a holy nation, a people belonging to God, that you may declare the praises of him who called you out of darkness into his wonderful light. (1 Peter 2:9)

Evangelism isn't just the role of an individual 'specialist' or a 'solo effort'. The church as a whole is a missionary body declaring together the praises of our Saviour and his message of reconciliation to the world. As Jesus says in John 17:21, when the world sees the unified witness of the church of Christ, they will believe.

Jesus was certainly convinced and compelled by love. He approached each day with a prayed-through and thought-through mission. People demanded that Jesus set up a hospital wherever he went, but despite the fact that everyone was looking for Jesus he moves on 'so I can preach the gospel there also. That is why I have come' (Mark 1:38).

Jesus tells all Christians to have the same intentional attitude. Why have I come to be here in this situation today? So I can preach the gospel here also, so that I can make disciples of all nations including this one, so I can invest today in work which will change a person's eternal destiny, so that by believing Jesus is the Christ you may have life in his name – for eternity, alleluia!

Because we have a wide range of options
(The 'idea overload' barrier to participation)

Romans is a good example of the Because Approach. Paul may not use the word 'because', but it's implicit in his great 'therefore' statements of chapters 8 and 12. Paul forces us to look beyond the glories of grace as a concept and ask the question 'So what?' So what for me as a person and for us as a church? The answer in Romans 12 is that God's people are to lead practical lives of worship, not just sing tuneful songs of worship:

– Because of the mercy God has shown to us, we sacrificially give our lives to doing God's perfect will (Rom. 12:1–2).

– Because of the grace God has given to each of us, we willingly carry out the activities God has apportioned us (Rom. 12:3–8).

Paul lists a number of activities in which a church will be involved. These include: prophesying; serving; teaching; encouraging; giving generously; leadership; acts of mercy. Paul's principle is simple: 'If he's got it...let him use it'. In the same way, every church is full of gifts and full of uses for those gifts.

So the question the church needs to ask is this: 'If we've got it...how should we use it?'

This is a difficult question to answer because there are so many possibilities and opportunities for a church – on Sundays and through the week, in church buildings and in the community, with Christians and those who are not yet Christians, with young and old...and so the list goes on. The solution is to discern the answers to these two fundamental questions:
1. What is our 'unique reason for being' (URB)?
2. What is our 'irreducible minimum' of outreach activities?

1. What is our 'unique reason for being' (URB)?
– If our church wasn't around anymore, what would people lack that they couldn't get elsewhere?
– What can we do that breaks new ground for the kingdom?
– What potential unbelievers can we reach that other churches can't reach as easily?
– How can we build up the Christians who are part of our church more effectively than other churches?

2. What is our 'irreducible minimum' of outreach activities?– What do we do to innovate church for all that is essential? What do we do that is merely helpful? What do we do that is unnecessary?
– If you had to rank all the activities you do as a church according to effectiveness of achieving your gospel purpose, what would be your top five? If you had to pick one activity from each of steps 2 to 5, which ones would you pick? What would your second choices be?

Step 4. Relevance building:			Step 5. Response building			Step 6. Participation:	
Secular	Uncertain	Boring	Identity	Mission	Call	Idea overload	Communication
Relevance building solutions			Response building solutions				

Because ignoring evangelism is not an option
(The 'communication' barrier to participation)

'What will it mean for the church to become the seeker? In the first place it will require the church to come to a fresh understanding that it is called to live not for itself but for the world that the Lord came to save. The church will need to review all its activities in the light of the great objective to be a sign and a servant of the kingdom of God in the world. It will mean facing a long list of hard questions, headed by the challenge, "Is there sufficient evidence within the confessing community that the King is indeed in residence among his people?"'[5]

A vicar I know in London used a novel way of teaching the church members to think about adapting to non-members. He spent a long time surveying the congregation, trying to find out what time they'd prefer to meet on a Sunday. At a major church meeting he got up and showed an analysis of the results. Then, he took the analysis and tore it up in front of everyone and said, 'of course, that's interesting but not determining. The more important question we need to ask as a church is when everyone in this area who doesn't come to church yet would like to come.'

The Lord's prayer begins with a vision of who God is and what his agenda is before we ask for anything for a reason. Jesus teaches us to seek first his kingdom rather than worrying about our comfort needs for a reason. The ACTS structure of prayer has the shopping list of Supplications at the end after prayers of Adoration, Confession and Thanksgiving for a reason. The reason is our tendency to think about ourselves before others, a tendency that can lead us to ignore our call to be Christ's ambassadors of the gospel. We are people who know life in relationship with God but can become so self absorbed that we fail to do the loving thing and share that life with others.

Mark Mittelberg talks about 'evangelistic entropy'. The second law of thermodynamics states that when left to itself, everything in the physical universe moves towards disorganization:
'In the same way the second law of spiritual dynamics is that all of us in the Christian community, if left to ourselves, move toward spiritual self-centredness.'[3]

A priority for any church is to be an evangelism base station – transmitting Christ's message of reconciliation by sending out Christians as ambassadors of the gospel. But effective gospel transmission starts with a fully functioning and powered base station.
'The [church's] first mission is always the internal mission: the church evangelized by the Holy Spirit again and again in the echoing word of Jesus inviting us to receive the reign of God and to enter it.'[4]

The problem for a company is always who to focus on pleasing – should it be the employees, customers, shareholders or suppliers? In the same way a church needs to work with the sometimes competing demands of staff, donors, members, visitors, ministry supply organisations and potential new members. With all the demands, the needs of the non-member can get a little overlooked – after all they don't have a seat or even a voice on any decision making group.

165

Solutions for individuals

Gain a gospel urgency

The more we understand the gospel's implications, the keener we will be to explain it to our friends.

For example, we see the Apostle Paul's motivation for proclaiming the gospel in passages such as Acts 17:16. Paul doesn't marvel at the buildings in Athens, nor is he impressed by the people's wisdom – he is greatly distressed by their spiritual bankruptcy.

We need to see afresh the height of God's love and the depth of our sin so that we're prepared to encourage our friends with the wonder of grace and warn them about the horror of judgement.

Know your gospel calling

Each of us has a unique role to play for God as his ambassadors of reconciliation.

Do you know and celebrate:

– The gospel situations in which God has placed you alone, where you can witness to him?

– The particular compassion towards lost people that God has placed within you?

– The personality and abilities God has given you which help you to develop gospel conversations?

What evangelism style[6] do you have (see below)? How does your style complement the styles of others in your small group or ministry service team?

Willow Creek's 6 Evangelism Styles applied to the Because Approach process

Interpersonal style	Invitational style Serving style	Testimonial style Intellectual style	Confrontational style
Relationship building.	Respect building.	Relevance building.	Response building.

Solutions for churches

1. Agree what you are called to do and not to do in the next few years (Knocking down the 'idea overload' barrier)

A. Agree which barriers to faith are the most vital to tackle in your setting

There is a limit to how many new initiatives can be started at any one time, so choose the barrier(s) you will focus on breaking down in the short- to medium-term based on:

– The analysis of your situation you have done so far concerning which are the biggest barriers to people progressing on the journey of faith in your setting
– The resources of the church you can call on without overstretching or overcomplicating
– The progression: there is no point tackling a barrier near the end of the journey of faith if a barrier farther back in the journey is still standing strong. Start as far back as necessary.

B. Agree which new initiatives you will begin and when

Of all the ideas and plans you have formed as you have gone through each stage of the Because Approach, which should you begin first?

Prioritize activities that:
– Knock down the earliest and biggest barriers to faith identified in the previous section 'A'
– Maintain a balance of relationship, respect, relevance and response building activities
– Contribute to your 'unique reason for being' (see page 164)
– Are 'irreducible minimums' for your church (see page 164)
– Ensure that you are going into your communities, not just expecting people to come into your buildings – 'go', don't just 'gather'.

Which should you plan to start in one, two or three years' time in order to follow people's progress on the journey of faith and fill in the gaps of barrier busting?

Solutions for churches

2. Develop a communication strategy (Knocking down the 'communication' barrier)

A. Appoint an evangelism point person

Mark Mittelberg[7] suggests that every church appoint an 'evangelism point person' who will:
– Model a life of personal evangelism to others. For example, in speaking to the church or teaching the Bible they may use illustrations from conversations they've had to show people it can be a natural part of any friendship.
– Teach and cast a vision for the value of evangelism until the church is 'institutionally evangelistic'.
– Keep the value central in the church leadership's thinking so that making the church more effective at sharing the gospel is always a factor in the planning of new initiatives.
– Get a team of people together who share a heart for the lost and have particular evangelism gifts. Train the team to be a resource to church members, groups or ministries organizing evangelistic activities.
– Nominate evangelism advocates in small groups and ministry teams and communicate with them about what they should be passing on to their group and praying about as a group.
– Organize a comprehensive strategy of events (see parts C to E for more details).
– Cast a vision for events centrally organized by the church.
– Tell stories of how events went to encourage and inspire people for next time.
– Encourage workers in the harvest field.

B. Agree a method of praying for your evangelism initiatives

– A regular slot at gatherings for believers (prayer meetings / services)
– Appoint specific groups / individuals to pray, and supply them regularly with prayer requests and updates
– Prayer at church small groups.

C. Establish a cycle of events

Link activities together in a progression:

a. Start with relationship and respect building activities which develop contact with people and show that Christians are not weird.

b. Then organize relevance building events that show how the Bible and Christianity make sense of the issues people face.

c. Finally, hold response events that enable people to look at the claims of the gospel and accept Christ as Lord.

It's important to remember that people don't like being processed like peas and may not be ready at the right time for a 'one size fits all' annual evangelism course. So offering opportunities throughout the year to explore Christian faith:

– Gives greater flexibility of choice with more entry points

– Means there is never too long a gap before someone connecting with Christianity can explore Christ further

– Is a powerful reminder that evangelism is core to the church throughout the year.

Option 1: A cycle of relationship, respect and relevance building activities each term that lead to an evangelistic course each term.

| January to Easter | Easter to August | September to December |

Option 2: In an annual cycle, focus on one or two activities each term: spring-term training for Christians and activities to establish relationships with unbelievers; summer-term activities that develop those relationships, show faith in practice and invite friends to relevance building events (one church calls this term 'let's barbecue'); during the autumn term invite friends to launch events for the evangelistic course (relevance building activity) and to the course itself (response building activity). Obviously some activities (such as a respect building toddler group) would still continue all year round.

| January to Easter | Easter to August | September to December |

169

Strategy expertise	Strategy process	Isolated	Liquid	Multi choice	Weird	Insular	Hypocritical

Preparation solutions	Relationship building solutions	Respect building solutions

D. Communicate your cycle of events

Describe your church's cycle in a form that is easy to remember and communicate.

The clearer people in the church are about what the process is, the clearer they will be about:
– Where in the cycle the church is
and therefore
– Who the upcoming events are for
and therefore
– Who they should think and pray about inviting and bringing to the next event
and therefore the more effective they will be at bringing people at various stages to appropriate events.

Methods for communicating these stages include:
– A regular slot at gatherings for believers (prayer meetings / services)
– A newsletter or email to all church members or to group and ministry team leaders
– Special prayer gatherings at the start of a cycle of activities.

Case studies

At Bellevue Baptist church[8] each church member is given a fishing tackle box packed full of resources to help them share their faith with friends. One resource is the Operation NetWork F.I.S.H. strategy:
Find who God wants you to reach.
Involve yourself in their lives (people don't care what you know till they know that you care).
Share your faith and your church and invite them to a special event.
Help them grow and reproduce (to not just be disciples, but disciplemakers).

At Willow Creek Community Church[9] members are taught seven steps from sinner to saint:
1. Build a relationship
2. Share a verbal witness
3. Invite to a seeker service
4. Become part of New Community (a midweek teaching and worship service for Christians)
5. Participate in a small group
6. Serve in the body of Christ
7. Steward financial resources.

Suggested model

One way of thinking about the cycle is in terms of the Christian life as a race[10] (Heb. 12:1).
The aim is to help potential runners on the long journey to get to the running track and, once they push off the starting blocks, to encourage those who run the Christian race to reach the prize of rest in the new creation (1 Cor. 9:24).

Stage 1: Meeting point

Before people enter the stadium they need to hear that the stadium exists, that there's a race going on and where they can see it.
Aim: Make contact with people who know nothing of Christianity.

Stage 2: Pre-match hospitality tent

Before people start to watch the race they are invited to meet up with some of the athletes in a hospitality tent to find out a bit about what the race entails and see that the athletes are OK people to be around.
Aim: Spend time with unbelievers and invite them to events where they will meet other Christians and see that they're not weird but know a loving God.

Stage 3: Back of the stands

Invite people to watch the race at first from a safe and anonymous distance.

Aim: Before explaining the core gospel, show that the Bible makes sense of the issues faced day by day. Show this through sharing a personal testimony or inviting to an event or course that will explain the Bible's teaching on a contemporary issue.

Stage 4: Front of the stands

Encourage people to take a closer look at the race and then get onto the track and off the starting blocks.

Aim: Explain the gospel and lead people to make a commitment through events and conversations.

Stage 5: Off the starting blocks

Run the race with other Christians to reach the prize of the new creation.

This picture of the race can help people visualise and understand ,ore clearly the overall process that underpins your church's outreach strategy. It also provides a 'shorthand'. For example:
– 'this is a hospitality tent event' tells people that there won't be a full blown gospel presentation but simply the opportunity to introduce friends who are not yet Christians to friends who are
– 'this is a front of the stands event' tells people that the friends they take will hear the gospel message and gospel challenge fair and square.

Other pictures that are less sports driven include a car gearbox[11] - going up the gears from 1 to 5, with each gear gaining more gospel momentum and the possibility of going down a gear if the going gets tough.

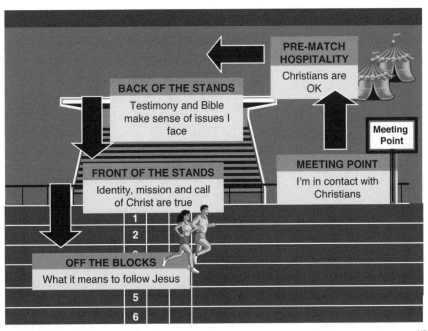

Step 1. Preparation.		Step 2. Relationship building.			Step 3. Respect building.		
Strategy expertise	Strategy process	Isolated	Liquid	Multi choice	Weird	Insular	Hypocritical
Preparation solutions		Relationship building solutions			Respect building solutions		

E. Form and cast an overarching vision

A vital part of communicating your evangelism process will be showing how it is key to your overall vision as a church.

Mission answers the question 'Why do we exist?' and is rooted in the same principles of Scripture for everyone. Vision answers the question 'Where are we called to go?' and will be specific to the situation in which Christ has placed each of his churches. As a result, vision statements develop as the situation develops while a mission statement remains the same for ever and for everyone.

The overarching vision statement for your church will come out of the analysis of the situation God has given you and the solutions you've decided on in the Because Approach. To form a vision statement, take time to pray together and seek the 'divine disturbance' within you – the driving passion to make a difference and change the situation of people for Christ's eternal glory. Ask:

1. In light of the situation God has placed us in and the activities God has called us to, what role has God given our particular church in building his kingdom?
– Your 'unique reason for being' (see p164).

2. In the light of the solutions we've decided on, what impact is our particular church going to make to God's kingdom in the future?
– Your 'irreducible minimums' (see p164).

There are several ways of casting vision:

a. A written document / brochure that everyone receives when they join the church which describes the exciting journey the church is heading on and why.

b. A vision event once a year where the whole church gets together to look back at how far they've come, what God's done and what he will do. This is almost a 'telling of inspiring stories of a hoped-for future round a campfire' – except it's likely to be done inside in an auditorium with a projector! But that doesn't need to stop it being a time where young and old dream dreams together.

c. A vision update from the church leader in the form of a letter sent personally to church members and/or published in a church magazine.

d. A vision update slot at each church prayer gathering.

e. Mottos (also called slogans or 'strap lines') express a particular strategic intent or goal. They sum up part of the vision of a church at one specific point in its strategic development. Mottos therefore change over time as the vision of that particular church develops.

F. Collate and communicate your values

Study guides 2-5 have all suggested writing specific value statements relating to the church's task of innovating church for all. Gather these statements together and place in a vision document.

People follow vision. The clearer a church's vision is, the more ready people will be:

– To join the church ('that's a people with a vision I want to be a part of')

– To get involved ('that's a vision I'll give my time, energy and money to')

– To stay involved when things are difficult ('this is the vision I've given my life to')

– To remain committed even when your preferred solution isn't chosen ('I'm committed to this vision because it's bigger than me and we own it together').

Examples of mottos
At St James Clerkenwell we began by using the following motto in internal communications: 'to be a church that reaches the people other churches cannot reach'. It made the point in the early days that our reason for building yet another church in central London was to reach into uncharted waters rather than fishing where other churches were already being effective.
To make another point we used the following motto in our external publicity 'a church for the whole community of Clerkenwell'.

Expert witness

Interview with J John, Philo Trust

What do you think are the main barriers that prevent individuals from having a passion to reach their lost friends?
Lack of enthusiasm, which surprises me, as the Greek word for enthusiasm is 'en – theos', or 'in God'... So how is it possible to be in God and not be enthusiastic?! I think also bad models of evangelism have somehow become barriers to using good models; there is a fear of causing offence.

What do you think are the main barriers preventing churches from having a passion to reach people with the gospel of Christ?
Making it first a priority; it has a maintenance mentality. The church is about three things: 'Look Up – Worship'; 'Look In – Welfare'; 'Look Out – Mission'. There is an imbalance in most churches, both in manpower and resources – most is spent on worship and welfare.

What helps people become more effective ambassadors of the gospel?
To see that they have a responsibility and that evangelism should be 'normal' for them; to see that they need to cultivate the web of relationships they already have.

What helps churches become more rescue focused?
Becoming intentional: when leaders, pastors and ministers carry out their responsibilities 'as if they were evangelists' (i.e. Paul's exhortation to Timothy), then this has influence on the flock.

What helps you keep your passion for evangelism?
The love of Christ. A missionary is not someone who crosses the sea, a missionary is someone who sees the cross – and is constantly sowing seed into the lives of the lost and seeing lives touched and transformed.

Study Guide 6.

Study Scripture Revelation 21:1–27
Where is the church heading?
Where are those outside God's forgiven family heading?

SCRIPTURE

SETTING

SOLUTION

3

Apply: What difference does knowing those final destinations make to your vision for the work to which God is calling your church?

Study Scripture 1 Peter 2:4–17
What role has Christ given his church in the world?

Apply: To what extent does your church's vision reflect this God-given role? How do your current activities and future plans reflect this God-given role?

Summary of Values
Gather your evangelism values from study guides 2 to 5 and incorporate into your vision communication documents and presentations.

We build relationships with people because Scripture says...

We are showing compassion in our communities because Scripture says...

We relate Christianity to daily life because Scripture says...

We explore the gospel with people because Scripture says...

Participation.

Analyse your setting

1. Review the list of your church's current activities in Study Guide 1 and initiatives for the future highlighted in Study Guides 2-5. Map existing and potential activities:

– Relationship Building activities

– Respect Building activities

– Relevance Building activities

– Response Building activities.

2. Analyse activities listed above

Highlight activities listed that are part of your 'Unique Reason for Being' (p164, 172)

Highlight activities listed that are part of your 'Irreducible Minimum'? (See p164, 172)

Highlight activities listed that are not part of your URB or IM are still important.

Highlight activities listed which are unnecessary.

Where are there still gaps? Do these need filling? If so, how will you fill them?

Which barriers will you make it your priority to break down first?

Prioritize activities above by contribution to the knocking down the key barriers to faith in your setting:

Priority 1	Priority 6
Priority 2	Priority 7
Priority 3	Priority 8
Priority 4	Priority 9
Priority 5	Priority 10

Participation solutions.

SCRIPTURE
SETTING
SOLUTION
3

Discuss and decide solutions
1. Goals
List activities planned and the year you will begin it:
– Relationship Building activities

– Respect Building activities

– Relevance Building activities

– Response Building activities

2. Strategies
How will you help each church member have a gospel urgency and a clear idea of their calling as part of the church's evangelism?

How can you build a rescue culture amongst members of the church?
Will you appoint an evangelism point person, and with what brief?

How will you maintain prayer as the powerhouse of your strategy?

How will you ensure evangelism is a '365' activity at your church?
What invitation cycle will you adopt?

How will you communicate the various stages of your strategy to people so they know the purpose of each activity and where each fits within the whole process?

How will you encapsulate and communicate your overarching vision?

Agree one or more concise and memorable mottos that sum up what you'd like your particular church to be known for.

[1] Used by kind permission of J John, Philo Trust.

[2] Bill Hybels at Willow Creek Association conference (Birmingham, 1999).

[3] The styles of evangelism were developed by the Willow Creek Association. See 'The Contagious Christian' course material: Mark Mittelberg, Lee Strobel and Bill Hybels, *Becoming a Contagious Christian: Participant's Guide* (Grand Rapids: Zondervan, 1995).

[4] Mark Mittelberg, *Building a Contagious Church: Revolutionizing the Way We View and Do Evangelism* (Grand Rapids: Zondervan, 2000).

[5] Darrell L. Guder (ed.), *The Missional Church* (Grand Rapids: Eerdmans, 1998).

[6] Gibbs and Coffey, *Church Next*.

[7] Mark Mittelberg, *Building a Contagious Church*

[8] www.bellevue.org.

[9] *Participating Membership Handbook* (Willow Creek Community Church, South Barrington, IL, USA).

[10] This idea is now also used with permission by Christians in Sport (christiansinsport.org.uk).

[11] Idea of Tim Crook, Associate Minister, St Peter's Church, Harold Wood

Innovating church for all. **Strategic summary.**

step 1. Preparation.

Mission statement:

	step 2. Relationship building.	step 3. Respect building.
Values	We build relationships with people because Scripture says...	We are showing compassion in our communities because Scripture says...

	Liquid	Multi choice	Isolated	Weird	Insular	Hypocritical
Key barriers to be knocked down						

	Relationship building solutions	Respect building solutions
Exsting activities retained		
Planned activities (Y1 - 20)		
Planned activities (Y2 - 20)		
Planned activities (Y3 - 20)		

step 6: Participation.

Outreach vision statement:

Outreach motos:

step 4: Relevance building.	step 5: Response building.
We relate Christianity to daily life because Scripture says...	We explore the gospel with people because Scripture says...

Secular	Uncertain	Boring		Identity	Mission	Call

Relevance building solutions	Response building solutions

Cycle of events:

January to Easter   Easter to August   September to December

A final word

Wisdom in the Bible is not about accumulating knowledge but about applying knowledge in action. I can have the most brilliant strategy imaginable but if it just remains imaginable then it's totally ineffectual.

The thoughts and ideas sparked in your mind, written on flip charts and drawn up in presentations as you have followed through the Because Approach will be exciting catalysts of change in your church when applied in action with:

– Discernment of what God might be asking you to do at the moment which is infused with realism as well as vision and ambition.
(If you try to do more than a few of the ideas here you will blow up!)

– Compassion for lost people fuelled by a clear view of their predicament and needs
(Without a mission imperative the game's up!)

– Authenticity in living the life of holiness and growth in Christ-likeness we are encouraging others to start living.
(Without a gospel life our communication will lack a gospel voice.)

BECAUSE 3

The Because Approach is about helping churches discern how Jesus wants to build their unique expression of church in their unique setting.

In Matthew 16:18 Jesus says, 'I will build my church, and the gates of Hades will not overcome it'

...because my church knows from my word why they're doing what they're doing

...because each member of my church knows what particular activities they're called to do in their particular setting

...because my church has a creative plan to do what they're called to do.